THE PRUDENT INVESTMENT ADVISER RULE™:

Risk and Liability Management
Strategies for Investment Fiduciaries

James W. Watkins, III, J.D., CFP®, AWMA®
InvestSense, LLC

ISBN: 9781530333578

Printed in the United States of America

TABLE OF CONTENTS

Chapter 1

Fiduciary 101

Asset allocation and investment advice have become integral parts of the financial planning and the wealth management industries. While financial planners and investment advisers (collectively, "investment advisers") may debate asset allocation's actual contribution to overall investment success and the best asset allocation computer software programs ("software programs") to use, most agree that the concept of asset allocation is a valuable wealth management technique.

Overlooked, however, is the fact that wealth management and investment advice, as practiced by some investment advisers, can result in imprudent investment advice for a client and liability exposure for the investment adviser. The purpose of this publication is to discuss the fiduciary traps that asset allocation and investment advice can create and some of the techniques investment advisers can use to avoid such fiduciary traps.

Due to the special issues involved with ERISA accounts, this publication will only look at investment advisers in a non-ERISA context. The Department of Labor is currently in the process of revising existing rules and regulations in order to provide better protection for pension plan participants and beneficiaries, including a uniform fiduciary standard that would require that anyone providing investment advice to a plan, participant and/or beneficiary must always put those parties' best interests first.

Industry Legal Standards

Investment advisers are fiduciaries by law.[1] Just like any other professional, investment advisers must take the time to determine what laws, regulations and legal standards are applicable to their profession.

Fiduciary law is based largely on common law trust and agency law. The courts have consistently held that the fiduciary standard is the "highest standard of care at law or equity,"[2] requiring "[n]ot honesty alone, but the punctilio of an honor the most sensitive...."[3]

Two of the primary duties of a fiduciary are the duty of loyalty and the duty of prudence. The duty of loyalty requires that a fiduciary always act in the best interests of their client. ERISA and the courts have developed a three prong test to determine if a fiduciary has breached their duty of loyalty, a test which is equally applicable in any fiduciary situation. The three questions are:

(1) Is there a conflict of interest that makes it impossible for the fiduciary to act with an eye singly to the beneficiaries' interests?
(2) If there is no conflict between the interests of the fiduciary and the interests of the plan participants and beneficiaries, has the fiduciary engaged in an extensive and independent investigation of options to ensure that the action taken was in the beneficiaries' best interest?
(3) Does the use of the trust's assets track the best interest of another party?[4]

The duty of prudence is self-explanatory. Under the Restatement (Third) Trusts Prudent Investor Rule, a fiduciary is held to a "prudent man/ investor" standard when managing a client's assets.[5] The Prudent Investor Rule and the Uniform Prudent Investor Act will be discussed in more detail in a later chapter.

Investment advisers who are also registered representatives of a broker-dealer are subject to FINRA Rules 2010 and 2310 ("Rule 2310"). FINRA Rule 2010 is perhaps the most powerful FINRA Rule. Often referred to as FINRA's "long arm" statute, Rule 2010 is drafted in such a way that FINRA can address any activity that it deems to be fraudulent, dishonourable or unfair. FINRA Rule 2010 is essentially the investment industry's version of Rule 206 of the Investment Advisers Act of 1940, as both are meant to allow the regulators to protect the public against abusive practices by those providing investment related services to the public.

FINRA Rule 2310 requires registered representatives to make reasonable efforts to obtain information from a client prior to making any investment recommendations and to only recommend investments that are prudent for that client based upon the client's financial needs, investment objectives, risk tolerance level and other personal investment parameters.

FINRA Interpretive Material 2310-2 describes some specific situations that have been deemed to be violations of Rule 2310, but cautions that the examples are not all-inclusive and that each case is determined on its specific facts and circumstances. In cases where a client refuses to provide any information, an investment adviser who decides to make any investment recommendations does so at their own risk, as the courts and the regulators have generally held that investment advisers who act without sufficient client information cannot satisfy the "reasonable grounds" requirement of Rule 2310.

All investment advisers, whether FINRA registered or not, must comply with the prudence requirements set out in the applicable investment adviser rules and regulations. Most states have enacted investment adviser rules and regulations that track both the Investment Adviser Act of 1940 ("Act") and the regulations promulgated pursuant to the Act.[6]

Interestingly enough, the Act itself does not actually contain an express prudence requirement. However, the courts and the regulators have held that Section 206 of the Act, which contains the Act's anti-fraud provisions, implicitly establishes both a prudence and fundamental fairness requirement.[7]

Section 206 provides that
> It shall be unlawful for any investment adviser, by use of the mails or any other means or instrumentality of interstate commerce, directly or indirectly:
> (1) to employ any device, scheme or artifice to defraud any client or prospective client;
> (2) to engage in any transaction, practice, or course of business which operates as a fraud or deceit upon any client or prospective client;...
> (3) to engage in any act, practice, or course of business which is fraudulent, deceptive, or manipulative...."[8]

While Rule 206 technically only applies to federally registered investment advisers and their investment advisory representatives, are deliberately ambiguous in nature in order to give the regulators the flexi-bility to address any situation that they feel needs to be addressed. One interesting aspect of Section 206 is the similarity of its language to that of Rule 10b-5[9] under the Securities Exchange Act of 1934.[10] Rule 10b-5 is often used in fraud actions against investment advisers.

Section 206 and the rules and regulations of the various securities related regulatory bodies do not create a private cause of action for investors. However, such laws, rules and regulations can be used in civil proceed-ings to establish the requisite standard of care required of investment ad-visers.[11]

The broad, general language of Rule 206 does not offer much in terms of objective prudence guidelines. In 1994, the Securities and Exchange Commission proposed an amendment to Section 206 that would have ex-pressly established a prudence/prudence requirement for investment ad-visers.[12]

For the most part, the proposed amendment mirrored the prudence re-quirements of Rule 2310. The proposed amendment was never adopted, as all parties agreed that a prudence requirement was already implicit in the Act. However given the proposed amendment's similarity to Rule 2310, FINRA decisions in enforcement actions may provide investment advisers with some valuable guidance as to applicable prudence guide-lines.

In summary, there are various rules and regulations that require invest-ment advisers to deal fairly with their clients by only recommending pru-dent investments, by making proper disclosure of the risks associated with such recommendations, and by not engaging in any activity that acts to defraud, deceive or manipulate their clients. The investment adviser is still left with little in the way of objective standards or examples to help them comply with such requirements.

Asset Allocation and Modern Portfolio Theory
Most investment advisers use software programs to produce their asset allocation recommendations. The majority of these software programs

are based on a financial theory known as Modern Portfolio Theory ("MPT"), which was first introduced by Harry Markowitz in 1952.[13]

MPT is based on a number of assumptions dealing with the correlation of investment returns, the value of diversification and the behavior of investors. The primary principle behind MPT is simple enough, namely diversification of a portfolio's assets in order to reduce a portfolio's overall risk and to improve the efficiency of a portfolio's overall performance. The principle remains valid today. It is the application, or more appropriately the misapplication, of the principle that has resulted in fiduciary liability traps for investment advisers.

The bear market that began in March of 2000 has brought to light many of the problems created by the misapplication of MPT, problems which were hidden by the incredible bull market of the 1990's. Investor complaints are at record levels. As a result, the integrity and continued value of asset allocation has been questioned by many.

Dr. William Sharpe, who won a Nobel Prize for his work with MPT and his own corollary, the Capital Asset Pricing Model, has even gone as far as to refer to the current misapplication of MPT and the resulting improper asset allocation practices as "financial planning in fantasyland."[14] Unfortunately, in many cases he may be correct, as financial planning and asset allocation have simply become marketing tools, with little or no regard for the quality of advice being provided.

This point has not been lost on the legal community. Attorneys are rapidly becoming aware of the ways that MPT has been, and continues to be, misapplied, as well as the inherent limitations of the software programs often used by investment advisers in the asset allocation process. Armed with this new understanding and in- formation, it is only a matter of time before the investors' bar fully advances new theories of liability to hold investment advisers to an even higher standard of care.

An example of this can be seen in one case, where the court ruled that the question of whether an investment adviser has a legal obligation to implement in a manner that is consistent with their original asset allocation recommendations/representations to a client is a genuine issue of fact that must be decided by a jury or other trier of fact.[15] While this decision involves just one court, it is still significant since it establishes a precedent that other courts and regulators can follow.

From the investment adviser's perspective, this decision is also significant in that many investment advisers cannot, or do not, perform a post-implementation analysis based on the client's actual and/or recommended investments. As Dr. William Sharpe has pointed out

> In a typical two-stage approach, the preferred asset allocation is selected on the assumption that all funds will be invested in passive and costless index funds. But actual investment vehicles typically have costs, added risks, and more complex relationships with the underlying asset classes. The result is likely to be inferior portfolio choices and overly optimistic forecasts of future performance.
>
> A far more rational approach uses only one stage, dealing directly with actual investment vehicles, with all their attractive and unattractive features.[16]

Using the reasoning presented in this case and Dr. Sharpe's observations, an investment adviser's failure to do such a post-implementation, or "real world," analysis to ensure both the consistency and the prudence of their investment recommendations could result in liability for the investment adviser based on theories such as negligence, breach of fiduciary duty and fraud.

The Prudent Investment Adviser Rule™
The combination of investment adviser laws/regulations and decisions of the courts and the regulators has produced various standards that, collectively, could be considered akin to a general Prudent Investment Adviser Rule™. There are obviously too many possible scenarios to fashion one

rule of prudent investment adviser behavior. Nevertheless, some fundamental standards appear on such a regular basis that if a Prudent Investment Adviser Rule™ were to be written, it would include the following provisions:

(1) An investment adviser owes each client a duty of loyalty and utmost good faith, and shall always act in the best interests of the client.

(2) In making investment recommendations, an investment adviser shall

(a) only recommend investments for which they have a reasonable basis to believe that the investments are prudent for the client based on the client's investment profile (e.g., investment objectives, risk tolerance level) and the client's financial situation, goals and needs;

(b) respect and act in accordance with a client's investment profile and desired course of action unless such profile and course of action are imprudent for the client, in which case the investment adviser shall advise the client of such prudence concerns and shall not participate in any implementation of such course of action;

(c) only make recommendations based on actual information about the client and not based on assumptions, presumptions and other guesswork;

(d) not make any recommendations if the investment adviser knows, or should know, that the client information they have is incomplete, inconsistent or suggests an imprudent course of action, in which case the investment adviser shall consult with the client to resolve such issues;

(e) not employ or engage in any scheme, act, transaction, practice, or course of conduct which operates as fraud, deceit, or manipulation upon any client or prospective client;

(f) ensure that all investment related recommendations including asset allocation recommendations/projections and all specific product recommendations, are consistent and do not otherwise mislead, defraud or deceive a client;

(g) personally disclose and explain to the client the risks associated with each investment recommendation and do so in a manner to ensure that the client truly understands such risks;

(h) personally disclose to the client all actual and potential conflicts of interest associated with such recommendations, including, but not limited to, and any commissions, compensation or other financial benefits the investment adviser may receive as a result of such investment recommendations.

(3) In assessing the prudence of an investment recommendation, an investment adviser shall

(a) make a customer specific determination of prudence for each investment recommendation;

(b) ensure that each separate investment recommendation satisfies the applicable legal prudence standard;

(c) consider both the client's indicated willingness and ability to bear risk, as well as the client's prior investing experience, age, investment time horizon, investment objectives and other personal investment parameters in determining the client's acceptable risk tolerance level; and consider all relevant factors in assessing the client's financial situation (and needs, including, but not limited to, a client's current or potential need for income and/or liquidity.

These general standards are just the framework for the development of a much broader concept of a Prudent Investment Adviser Rule. Legislation and decisions in court and regulatory proceedings have added, and will continue to additional specifics to the general standards. To fully understand the rationale behind the concept of a Prudent Invest Adviser Rule™, it is necessary to understand the issues addressed by such a rule and the decisions/ developments that have helped shape such a rule.

Chapter 2

Development of the Prudent Investment Adviser Rule™

The Quality of Investment Advice Matrix™

Recommendations

		Imprudent	Prudent
Implementation	**Imprudent**	Imprudent Recommendations/ Imprudent Implementation	Prudent Recommendations/ Imprudent Implementation
	Prudent	Imprudent Recommendations/ Prudent Implementation	Prudent Recommendations/ Prudent Implementation

The Asset Allocation Quality of Advice Matrix™ ("Matrix") identifies the four possible scenarios that can result from an investment adviser's provision of asset allocation and investment recommendations and the implementation of such recommendations. Prudence, within the context of the Matrix, implies prudence both in terms of (1) a client's willingness and capacity to bear risk, and (2) the consistency between the investment adviser's original recommendations and any implementation of such recommendations. Given the unlikelihood of the imprudent recommendation/prudent implementation scenario occurring, we will focus on the three remaining scenarios.

The Prudent Recommendations/
<u>Prudent Implementation Scenario</u>

The prudent recommendations/prudent implementation scenario represents the ideal situation, where both the recommendations and any implementation are prudent for a client and any implementation is consistent with the investment adviser's original portfolio recommendations and representations. This scenario is only attainable when the investment adviser does the appropriate due diligence, both as to the generic asset allocation recommendations and the specific product recommendations, in order to ensure consistency and overall prudence. The remaining two scenarios will provide advice on how to achieve this scenario.

Chapter 3

Asset Allocation Fiduciary Prudence Traps

Traditional Asset Allocation Traps

While computer software programs make it easier for an investment adviser to generate asset allocation recommendations, such programs may
produce imprudent investment advice and unwanted liability exposure for
an investment adviser due to the nature of the software programs and the
fact that such software programs are often based on MPT. It is this combination of imprudent investment advice for the client, together with the
resulting liability exposure, that creates an asset allocation prudence trap
for an investment adviser.

Traditional asset allocation prudence traps can present them-selves in either one of two scenarios. In the first scenario, the asset allocation software program produces imprudent asset allocation recommendations and
the investment adviser, relying on such recommendations, implements in
an imprudent manner. The second scenario occurs when the asset allocation software program produces prudent asset allocation recommendations, but the investment adviser's implementation of such recommendations is imprudent.

The Imprudent Recommendations/
Imprudent Implementation Scenario

The first scenario often results from the fact that MPT is not the legal
standard for determining the prudence of investment advice in non-
ERISA accounts. The client's risk tolerance level is often the determining
factor in assessing the prudence of an investment adviser's investment
advice.

The courts and the regulators take the position that an investor's risk
tolerance level is absolute and that each investment in the investor's
portfolio will be evaluated for prudence based upon the investor's risk
tolerance level, investment objectives, financial needs and other personal investment parameters. MPT, on the other hand, takes the

position that an investor's risk tolerance level is relative and that prudence should be determined in the context of the overall performance of an investor's portfolio. This scenario may also result from an investment adviser's development of a "black box" mentality toward asset allocation or an investment adviser's inability to properly construct, constrain or interpret various asset allocation tools, such as risk tolerance questionnaires.

Modern Portfolio Theory

Most software programs rely on MPT to produce asset allocation recommendations. This reliance on MPT creates a potential prudence trap, as MPT is not, and never has been, the standard used by the courts and the regulatory bodies in assessing the prudence of fiduciary investment advice.[17] As a result, recommendations may be theoretically prudent under MPT and still be legally imprudent for a client, thus exposing a client to unnecessary risk and the investment adviser to potential legal liability.

There are those who argue that the legal standard for determining prudence is outdated and that MPT should be the sole standard for determining the prudence of investment advice. Proponents of this position often point to the fact that a number of states have adopted the Uniform Prudent Investor Act ("UPIA")[18] or the Prudent Investor Rule ("Rule")[19], both of which adopt an overall portfolio approach in assessing the prudence of investment advice.

Prudent Investor Rule that investment advisers should be aware of in order to protect themselves from liability. These points and misconceptions are discussed more fully later herein. For the time being, suffice it to say that such arguments are flawed. Regardless of whether one accepts or rejects such arguments, the fact remains that the legal prudence standard is the standard actually used in determining an investment adviser's liability for imprudent investment advice.

Given the fact that the legal prudence standard is derived from rules enacted pursuant to the Securities Act of 1934[20] and that no overwhelming reason has been shown to modify the provisions of such a significant piece of legislation, investment advisers need to understand the legal prudence standard and adjust their practices accordingly in order to protect both their interests and their clients' interests. The chances of MPT being adopted as the sole standard for determining the prudence of investment advice are even more unlikely in light of recent studies that appear to cast doubts on the viability of MPT based software programs and some of the key assumptions upon which MPT is based.[21]

One of the key principles of MPT is the combination of various types of assets in order to stabilize a portfolio's performance. The premise behind this principle is that by combining assets that behave differently in certain market conditions, the poor performance of some assets will be balanced out by the performance of other assets. However, recent studies have shown that in some cases, the correlation of returns among assets actually increases in times of volatility, thereby negating or significantly reducing the assumed benefits of correlation and diversification.[22]

Another obstacle to the adoption of MPT as the standard for investment advice prudence lies in its assumption that an investor's risk tolerance level is relative, meaning that an investor will always be willing to accept greater investment risk as long as the potential reward compensates the investor for the assumption of such risk. Proponents of the current legal prudence standard argue that this assumption leaves an investor with no adequate way to fully protect their financial interests, as it unilaterally adopts a dangerous assumption that in many cases may not be true.

Even Markowitz recognized the need to use MPT judiciously, with proper recognition of and allowance for an investor's personal investment needs, investment parameters and financial situation, by stating that

> the proper choice of criteria depends on the nature of the investor....For each type of investor the details of the portfolio analysis must be suitably selected....The proper choice among efficient port folios depends on the willingness and ability of the investor to assume risk.[23]

The combination of expected return and variance which promises the greatest return in the long run is not necessarily the combination which best meets the investor's needs. The investor may prefer to sacrifice long-run return for short-term stability.[24]

Investment advisers relying on MPT and/or MPT based software programs in providing financial advice should proceed cautiously in order to avoid giving clients legally imprudent investment recommendations.

Black Box" Wealth Management

Investment advisers who lack the necessary know-ledge, training or experience in financial planning and asset allocation to properly provide such services may develop a "black box" mentality. While such software programs can be a valuable tool in the asset allocation process, investment advisers must recognize they are just that, tools, a beginning point, and must be properly set-up and constrained in order to provide any value to the asset allocation process.

Investment advisers must guard against not only the theoretical prudence-legal prudence trap, but also against the use of questionable or invalid risk and return input data ("input data"). The use of questionable input data or the failure to properly constraint software programs may result in imprudent recommendations, the proverbial "garbage in, garbage out" syndrome.

This is particularly true with MPT based software programs due to MPT's inherent bias toward assets that combine high returns and low volatility with a low correlation to other assets.[25] Given The sensitivity of MPT based calculations to such numbers, slight modifications in just one or two numbers can result in significant differences in the asset allocation recommendations produced. This relative instability of MPT based software programs has led one expert to characterize such software programs as "estimation-error maximizers."[26]

Another issue regarding the validity and the viability of the input data used is the fact that traditional, MPT based asset allocation assumes that the returns, the standard deviations and the correlation of the investments or the asset classes remain static over time. Experience has shown that such investment performance numbers can fluctuate greatly based on any number of factors, from economic to psychological to pure greed.[27]

The Monte Carlo simulation techniques used by many investment advisers today not only recognize the randomness of such investment performance numbers, but also rely on such randomness in the calculation of the probability of various investment scenarios. The popularity of Monte Carlo simulation techniques may be a result of the liability issues created by MPT's static investment data assumption.

Properly used, MPT can be a useful tool for investment advisers in the asset allocation process. However, concerns over the validity and viability of the input data, the relative instability of the software program calculations, and the potential for unethical manipulation of such calculations are additional reasons why it is unlikely that MPT will be, or should be, adopted as the prudence standard for investment advice.

Risk Tolerance Questionnaires

Investment advisers often use risk tolerance questionnaires to assist them in the asset allocation process. While such questionnaires can sometimes provide helpful insight into a client's feelings and investment philosophy, investment advisers must also recognize the inherent limitations of such planning documents. Questionnaires can produce inaccurate and misleading analyses due to such factors as the wording of the questions, the weighting of the questions, the areas covered/omitted in the questionnaires, and the nature of the questions.

Proper analysis of such questionnaires is equally important in assessing a client's true risk tolerance level. Risk tolerance questionnaires typically produce a score based on an average or a cumulative score of all of the client's answers the questionnaire's questions. However, not all questions should be given equal weight, as certain factors (e.g., risk tolerance, investment objectives) always take priority in determining prudence.

Some investment advisers, and for that matter some compliance officers, may fail to perform proper analyses of risk tolerance questionnaires, choosing instead to take the expedient route of simply adopting the questionnaire's average or collective score. Unfortunately, this oversight often results in another asset allocation prudence trap for investment advisers. Proper analysis of risk tolerance questionnaires is discussed more fully in the Risk Tolerance section.

The Prudent Recommendations/
<u>Imprudent Implementation Scenario</u>

The next scenario is very common. The prudent recommendations/ imprudent implementation scenario results from inconsistencies, or gaps, between the investment adviser's original asset allocation recommendations and the implementation of such recommendations. Such gaps often result from a lack of due diligence by the investment adviser or the limitations of the software program used to produce the asset allocation recommendations.

As previously noted, investment advisers often use software programs to produce portfolio recommendations for clients. Due to the amount of data that is required to perform MPT based asset allocation calculations, most commercial software programs only generate recommendations in terms of broad, generic asset categories (e.g., large cap growth, small cap value), leaving the investment adviser with the task of selecting appropriate specific investment products to implement the recommendations.

Once the specific investment products are chosen, most software programs will not allow the investment adviser to go back and perform a post-implementation, or "real world," portfolio analysis based on the client's actual and/or recommended investments. An investment adviser's inability to verify the consistency between his original asset allocation recommendations and the investment portfolio actually implemented, to identify any recommendation-implementation gaps, creates potentially significant liability concerns for the investment adviser.

Asset allocation software programs falsely assume that all investment options/products in an asset category are equivalent to each other.[28] Investment advisers wanting to avoid liability for imprudent investment advice must recognize this inherent weakness and perform the due diligence necessary to ensure consistency between their asset allocation recommendations and their implementation recommendations.

Some investment advisers overlook or dismiss this inconsistency, simply assuming, as does MPT, that a client is willing to assume the additional risk as long as there is also an increased chance of greater returns. From a potential liability perspective, the problem with this practice is that the assumption may not reflect the client's true risk tolerance level and is not legally justified.

As the legal community learns more about MPT and the inherent limitations of asset allocation software programs, investment advisers should not be surprised to see the courts and the regulators impose liability on advisers when clients suffer losses due to the existence of such recommendation-implementation gaps. This would be consistent with the announced purpose of the securities laws, to protect the public against what may be perceived as fraudulent or deceptive practices, where the balancing of interests almost always favors the public.[29]

It has been suggested that these recommendation- implementation gaps can operate as a form of bait-and-switch, with the client being unfairly persuaded to make commission generating securities transactions through the use of optimistic risk/return projections in the investment adviser's asset allocation recommendations, only to receive an actual investment portfolio far different from the investment adviser's original recommendations and projections.

Along those same lines, it has been suggested that since an investment adviser knows that the products that will be recommended in the implementation stage have significant differences between the generic indices used in producing the computer produced recommendations, especially with regard to fees and other costs, the recommendations are essentially worth-less at best, and a potential violation of the antifraud provisions of Rule 10b-5.

Rule 10b-5 prohibits any person from
(a) employing any device, scheme, or artifice to defraud,
(b) making any untrue statement of a material fact or omitting to state a material fact necessary in order to make the statements made, in the light of the circumstances under which they were made, not misleading, or
(c) engaging in any act, practice, or course of business which operates or would operate as a fraud or deceit upon any person, in connection with the purchase or sale of any security.[30]

The argument is that since the investment adviser knows of the material differences between the representations in the recommendations and the actual products used in implementation, the investment adviser needs to either (1) provide a revised recommendation document based on the actual products used in implementation, or (2) provide the client with disclosure document informing them of the material differences in the original recommendations and the probable impact on the quality and performance of their implemented investment portfolio.

No one knows whether such arguments would be persuasive or not. Presumably, a pivotal issue would be whether, given the facts and the circumstances of a particular case, the investment adviser has a fiduciary obligation to a client to recommend specific investments for implementation that are consistent with the representations used to convince the client to make the portfolio changes. Rule 10b-5 applies to both fiduciary and non-fiduciary advisers.

In light of the uncertainty created by the previously discussed court opinion on this issue, the Prudent Investment Adviser™ will re-examine all aspects of their asset allocation practices and implementation practices.

The key point for the financial planning and investment advisory Industries is that such theories are being promoted and that the investment adviser's failure or inability to verify the absence of any recommendation-implementation gaps issue creates potentially serious liability issues for investment advisers.

The Active Management Value Ratio™:
Quantifying Prudence and Fiduciary Cost Control
A fund's cost inefficiency is another factor that often causes an investment to be deemed imprudent. Simply put, "wasting a client's money is never prudent."[31]

The key in evaluating the reasonableness of a mutual fund's fees and other costs is to compare the fee to the benefit received. The Active Management Value Ratio™ (AMVR), a proprietary metric of InvestSense, LLC, allows investors and investment fiduciaries to perform a simple cost/benefit efficiency analysis com-paring an actively managed mutual fund's incremental/added cost to the fund's incremental/added benefit.

The choice to use a fund's incremental cost and incremental return in analyzing an actively managed mutual fund is based on Charles Ellis' research and his conclusion that

> The real marginal cost of active management is the incremental fee that active managers charge versus the incremental returns they deliver.[32]

The most effective use of the AMVR is in comparing an actively managed mutual fund to a comparable benchmark, such as a passively managed index mutual fund or index-based exchange traded fund. In using the AMVR in my practices, it is recommended that the funds' five-year annualized returns be used in calculating incremental return in order to reduce the possibility of any skew by an outlier performance.

In computing incremental costs, I check both funds' current prospectus and use both funds' stated annual expense ratio and turnover ratio. Both ratios should be used in calculating the impact of both fund's incremental costs, based on research that has shown that "the two variables that do the best job in predicting [a mutual fund's] performance are expense ratios and turnover.[33]

Once the AMVR is calculated, the investment can interpret the AMVR score by asking two simple questions:

> (1) Does the actively managed fund provide an investor with any incremental return, i.e. outperform the benchmark used in calculating the fund's AMVR?
> (2) If actively managed fund does provide an incremental return, does the incremental return exceed the actively managed fund's incremental costs?

If the answer to either of these questions is "no", the actively managed fund is not a prudent investment option. If the answer to both of these questions is "yes," then the investment adviser can proceed with analyzing the fund on other criteria, such as consistency of performance and possible "closet index fund" status.

Monte Carlo Simulation Traps

Some investment advisers, recognizing the liability issues associated with traditional, MPT based asset allocation, have turned to Monte Carlo simulations to help them in the asset allocation process. The Monte Carlo simulation techniques used by many investment advisers today not only recognize the randomness of such investment performance numbers, but also rely on such randomness in their calculations.

Numerous potential investment scenarios are produced, along with the probability of such scenarios, and the client is usually asked to choose the one with which they would be most comfortable. Specific investment products are then recommended based upon the investment scenario chosen by the client.

Unbeknownst to many investment advisers, the use of Monte Carlo simulations to produce asset allocation recommendations present most, if not all, of the same prudence liability issues as the traditional software programs since risk and return assumptions are used and the same generic-to-specific implementation issues exist. Again, the issue would presumably be whether, given the facts and circumstances of a particular case, the investment adviser has a fiduciary obligation to recommend specific investments for implementation that are consistent with the original asset allocation recommendations and representations that were given to a client.

Consequently, investment advisers who believe that they can eliminate or limit their fiduciary duty regarding the prudence of their investment advice should be aware that

- the duty to recommend prudent investment advice is the investment adviser's alone and cannot be assigned to a client;[34]
- the use of exculpatory provisions, or "hedge clauses," that attempt to eliminate or limit an investment adviser's fiduciary duty liability may constitute fraud under the Act and result in the voiding of client advisory contracts;[35]
- a client's opinion as to the prudence of investment advice is not relevant in assessing the prudence of such advice;[36]
- investment advisers who know or should know that the client's investment objectives or indicated risk tolerance level are imprudent for the client may not rely on such errors and must inform the client of such imprudence.[37]

In short, an investment adviser using Monte Carlo simulations to produce investment recommendations can expect to be held to the same prudence standards as an investment adviser using traditional asset allocation techniques, both as to their generic and specific asset allocation and investment recommendations.

Third Party Asset Management Traps

Some investment advisers have decided to simply turn the asset allocation and the money management responsibilities over to third party money managers. In most of these programs, the third party money manager develops a number of model portfolios for a client to choose from.

The third party money manager then allocates the client's funds in accordance with the model portfolio chosen. The third party usually provides the investment adviser with new asset allocation recommendations periodically. The investment adviser then either approves or rejects the recommended portfolio changes or contacts the client to get the client's approval or rejection of the new asset allocation recommendation. These programs present special issues and challenges for investment advisers - two of which will be covered here.

The first issue is the same MPT asset allocation prudence issue previously discussed. In most cases, the third party money manager's asset allocation recommendations are an all-or-nothing proposition, with no modification allowed to address a client's personal investment objectives, risk tolerance level or other personal investment parameters. The problem with these generic one-size-fits-all asset allocation programs is that they often produce recommendations that may be theoretically acceptable, but they are often legally imprudent for a particular client, thus exposing the investment adviser to potential liability exposure.

Since the third party money manager receives its fee regardless of whether their recommendations are accepted or rejected, an investment adviser may feel a need to legitimize the third party money manager's fee by choosing recommendations that are, in fact, imprudent for a client. This can result in further liability exposure, which leads to the second issue, prudence determination liability.

As discussed earlier, an investment adviser is simply required to deal fairly with clients by only recommending prudent investments, by properly disclosing the risks associated with such recommendations and by not engaging in any conduct that could deceive or mislead clients. There is also no legal requirement that an investment adviser contract to do anything that could result in exposing themselves to unnecessary legal liability, which is exactly what such plans and projections often do due to the investment adviser's inability or failure to verify the lack of any recommendation-implementation gaps.

The third party money managers in such asset management programs are well aware of the prudence liability issue. If investment advisers carefully study their contracts with such third party money managers, they will notice that the contract usually states that that the investment adviser, not the third party money manager, is responsible for determining the prudence of both the third party money manager's overall program and all asset allocation recommendations provided. This contractual agreement, plus the fact that the third party money manager usually has no direct or contractual relationship with the investment adviser's client, effectively transfers all liability exposure for imprudent investment advice to the investment adviser.

All of this is perfectly legal and, to be honest, very shrewd. The problem is that many investment advisers are often unaware of either the existence or the significance of this contract provision, leading them to mistakenly assume that the third party money manager is determining the prudence of the asset allocation recommendations. In such cases, the end result is that no one is protecting the client's interests by ensuring the prudence of the asset allocation recommendations and the money management decisions.

Reducing Asset Allocation Liability Exposure
If you were to ask most investment advisers to describe their obligation to their clients, you would probably get responses such as "to obtain the maximum return for a given level of risk" or "to obtain the best return for a client," both of which are legally incorrect absent any contractual obligations to the contrary.

One method investment advisers might consider to potentially reduce liability for imprudent asset allocation recommendations is to use their software programs to produce legally prudent asset allocation recommendations, but not to distribute any documentation of the results or to state any risk/return projections. Unless the investment adviser contracts otherwise, neither the Act nor any other legal rule/regulation requires advisers to provide financial plans or asset allocation plans.

Investment advisers who do decide to use MPT based software programs, should concentrate on (1) properly constraining the asset allocation software program chosen so that the client's risk tolerance level, financial needs, investment objectives and other personal investment parameters are properly considered, and (2) verifying both the validity and viability of the input data to be used in generating the recommendations.

There are basically two schools of thought with regard to the issue of the validity and the viability of the input data. One school of thought takes the position that purely historical data should be used. The other school of thought believes that the data should include reasonable assumptions about future performance of the financial markets and the specific assets/asset categories.

From a liability perspective, the interjection of subjectivity usually increases the potential for liability exposure. This may be particularly true with MPT based asset allocation recommendations, where small errors can be significantly magnified due to the inherent bias of MPT toward certain types of assets. Under certain circumstances an over-statement of an asset's return and/or an understatement of an asset's risk could potentially be the basis for a potential fraud claim.

While the use of purely objective historical input data does not guarantee greater accuracy, it is probably more defensible in the event prudence questions arise. There is no specific historical time frame that is required to be used for the risk and return input data. Some believe that long time frames, such as 50 years or more, smooth out potential volatility issues and give a more accurate picture of the potential long term risks and returns of investing.

Others believe that shorter time frames, such as ten years, provide a more current, and thus more accurate, picture of reasonable risk and return expectations for an investor. Regardless of what time frame is used, the investment adviser must ensure that the input data used in the asset allocation process is accurate and does not otherwise invalidate the asset allocation recommendations or mislead the client.

An example of potential accuracy issues can be seen with regard to the use of historical yields. Given the recent trend of corporations to eliminate or to significantly reduce their dividend pay-outs, the use of long-term historical yield data could produce yield projections that significantly overstate the yield from the asset allocation recommendations. Such an error could result in liability exposure for the investment adviser in cases where a client has a financial need for or an investment objective of current income.

There are those who would claim that Rule 2310 should exempt an investment adviser from any liability if the client's trades are purely unsolicited. The "financial suicide" decisions suggest that the prudent decision may be to avoid any potential liability by refusing to participate in such activity.

Investment advisers are often frustrated by conservative clients who have the ability, but not the willingness, to bear investment risk. In light of recent events and disclosures concerning the stock market, such conservatism may become much more common. Investment advisers facing such situations must remember that, ultimately, it is the client's decision as to how to invest their assets.

Nevertheless, there have been cases where clients have attempted to hold investment advisers liable for investment advice that was claimed to be too conservative for the client. Consequently, in situations where a client chooses to disregard the investment adviser's advice and to invest in a much more conservative manner than his indicated willingness or ability to bear investment risk, the Prudent Investment Adviser™ should consider either

- having the client sign a document acknowledging what the investment adviser's investment recommendations were, that the client chose not to follow such recommendations, and that the investment adviser explained the risks associated with the client's desired course of conduct;
- sending the client a "prudence letter" afterward stating what the investment adviser's investment recommendations were, that the client chose not to follow such recommendations, and that the risks associated with the client's anticipated course of conduct were explained to the client; or
- at a minimum, preparing a file memo establishing these same elements.

While there is no guarantee that any of these strategies will insulate an investment adviser from liability, they should be useful in defending any "financial suicide" or, in this case, "reverse financial suicide" claim by showing that the investment adviser did in fact provide prudent investment advice, which was rejected by the client.

Assuming that these two steps are properly executed, the investment adviser must still choose prudent investment products to use in implementation and, equally important, verify the absence of any recommendation-implementation gaps. It has been suggested that investment advisers could perhaps protect themselves against recommendation-implementation gap liability by simply adding some disclaimer language to the client's contract and to all asset allocation documents.

Such disclaimer language would state that all recommendations and projections are based on historical data and that past performance does not guarantee similar performance in the future. Investment advisers may recognize this as basically the same disclosure language that is required in investment advertisements.

It is unclear whether such an approach would be successful. As noted earlier, the courts and the regulators do not look favorably on attempts by investment advisers to disclaim or limit their fiduciary liability for their advisory activities.[38] A key question in such a case would appear to be whether, given the facts and circumstances of a particular case, the investment adviser has a fiduciary obligation to recommend specific investments that will result in a final investment portfolio that is consistent with the asset allocation recommendations and projections that were used to persuade the client to make changes in their portfolio.

Investment advisers may find themselves in situations where a client does not want to follow the investment adviser's advice. In situations where a client wants to invest in a manner that exceeds either their indicated willingness or ability to bear investment risk, the investment adviser should counsel the client as to the imprudence of the client's desired course of action and explain to the client that legal guidelines dictate that the investment adviser cannot participate in such activity.

Investment advisers who provide asset allocation recommendations should read everything they can about asset allocation and portfolio optimization to gain a better understanding of the asset allocation process and the various theories that exist. In the event that prudence questions arise, the investment adviser can expect to be questioned about his knowledge and understanding of the process and such theories. Investment advisers who believe that they can avoid liability for imprudent investment recommendations by simply claiming that they relied on a software program will be disappointed.

Prudent investment advisers must navigate various legal minefields in order to ensure legal prudent investment recommendations and avoid unwanted asset allocation prudence liability. The most effective way for investment advisers to reduce potential liability exposure for imprudent investment advice is simply to listen to their clients and respect their client's indicated investment objectives, risk tolerance level, and other personal investment parameters unless the client's desired course of conduct is clearly imprudent for the client.

In some cases, investment advisers get so caught up with the theoretical and technological aspects of asset allocation, looking for the "optimal" investment portfolio, that they overlook the client's financial needs and wishes. As Markowitz himself cautioned, the "optimal" investment portfolio may not be the appropriate choice for an investor based upon the investor's risk tolerance level, financial needs and investment objectives.[39] By concentrating on only recommending legally prudent investments, an investment adviser can effectively protect both their interests and their clients' interests.

Investment advisers who are FINRA licensed should also note that conflict of interest issues still exist with regard to investment advisers who receive both commissions and fees in connection with managing client accounts, even when the adviser fully discloses the compensation arrangement to clients. The position of the courts and the regulators has been that such situations create an inherent conflict of interest that cannot be resolved by a simple disclosure since a client may not understand all of the issues involved.[4]

Chapter 4

Prudent Investor Rule Traps

In 1990, the American Law Institute restated portions of the Restatement (Second) of Trusts that dealt with investment guidelines for trustees. The restated portions, which came to be known as the Prudent Investor Rule ("Rule")[41], recognize the value of portfolio diversification and impose a duty on a trustee to diversify a trust's assets unless it would not be prudent to do so. The Prudent Investor Rule provides that

> [t]he trustee is under a duty to the beneficiaries to invest and manage the funds of the trust as a prudent investor would in light of the purposes, terms, distributions requirements, and other circumstances of the trust.
>
> (a) This standard requires the exercise of reasonable care, skill, and caution, and is to be applied to investments not in isolation but in the context of the trust portfolio and as a part of an overall investment strategy, which should incorporate risk and return objectives reasonably prudent to the trust.
>
> (b) In making and implementing investment decisions, the trustee has a duty to diversify the investments of the trust unless, under the circumstances, it is prudent not to do so.
>
> (c) In addition, the trustee must:
>> (1) conform to the fundamental fiduciary duties of loyalty and impartiality;
>> (2) act with prudence in deciding whether and how to delegate authority and in the selection and super-vision of agents; and
>> (3) incur only costs that are reasonable in amount and appropriate to the investment responsibilities of the trusteeship.
>
> (d) The trustee's duties under this Section are subject to the rule of §228, dealing primarily with contrary investment provisions of a trust or statute.[42]

This conservative position, commonly known as the Prudent Person Rule[43], is still the applicable trustee standard in most states that have not adopted the Prudent Investor Rule and in most non-trustee investment adviser situations. In situations where the Prudent Person Rule still applies, the prudence of a investment adviser's investment recommendations will be determined on the basis of the legal prudence standard's transactional approach (i.e. as to each individual investment) rather than the Prudent Investor Rule's overall portfolio approach.

The Rule, however, does not give investment advisers unfettered discretion regarding diversification. While the Rule endorsed the value of diversification, the drafters of the Rule deliberately did not endorse MPT or any other financial or economic theory regarding diversification[44], a significant fact that has been overlooked or ignored by many investment advisers, compliance officers and attorneys.

In fact, the comments to the Rule note the committee's opinion that such theories have legitimate questions and weaknesses.[45] In diversifying a trust's assets, the Rule requires that a trustee act prudently given the purposes, objectives and terms of the trust, including the risk and return objectives and financial needs of the trust's beneficiaries.

An investment adviser entitled to rely on the Rule can still face liability for imprudent asset allocation recommendations if the investment adviser cannot sufficiently justify the role or alleged benefits of such recommendations vis-à-vis the overall portfolio, or if it can be shown that the recommendations were not prudent when made due to the terms of the trust and/or the needs of the beneficiaries.[46] For example, an adviser who recommends primarily non-income or low income producing investments for a trust intended to provide income for its beneficiaries faces potential liability for imprudent investment recommendations.

Often overlooked is the fact that the Rule, as drafted in the Restatement (Third) of Trusts and in the statutes of the states that have adopted the

Rule, technically only applies to trustees, not to all investment advisers or fiduciaries. In most cases the courts have extended the Rule's coverage to include similar fiduciaries, such as guardians, executors and conservators.

Investment advisers hoping for a similar extension of the Rule to all investment advisers should not be overly optimistic, as there is no authority for such an extension. In endorsing the idea that trustees should have greater flexibility in managing trust investments, the drafters of the Prudent Investor Rule were considering trustees in the traditional sense, trustees with no securities or insurance licenses and the accompanying inherent conflict of interest issues.

Investment advisers also need to remember that the Rule did not adopt MPT or any other financial or economic theory as the legal standard for determining the prudence of asset allocation advice. In some cases, the diversification contemplated by the Rule could arguably be as simple as the traditional 60 percent equity/40 percent fixed income split, a 60 percent fixed income/40 percent equity split, or a 50 percent/50 percent split between a growth index fund and a value index fund. For more conservative investors, diversification may involve nothing more than recommending fixed income investments with various returns and maturities (e.g., laddering a bond portfolio or constructing a barbell bond portfolio).

Investment advisers who intend to rely on the Rule should review the laws and regulations of the state involved in order to determine whether the state has enacted the Rule and, if so, whether the investment adviser's proposed activities are covered under the state's interpretation of the Rule. In most states that have adopted the Rule, the applicable provision will be found in the laws and regulations pertaining to trusts and trustees.

Investment advisers who are dually registered i.e., also registered representatives of a broker-dealer, should note that in assessing the prudence of their investment advice, FINRA and SEC rules and regulations always take priority over the Rule. This is extremely significant since the regulators and the courts continue to determine the prudence of an investment adviser's investment advice with regard to each individual investment, not in the context of the overall performance of an investment portfolio.

Chapter 5

The Search for Fiduciary Prudence Guidelines

Laws and regulations are often written in broad, general terms in order to provide flexibility in enforcement. Those looking for more definitive, more specific guidelines often have to look at rulings and decisions involving such laws and regulations. Such is generally the case with regard to prudence guidelines for investment advisers.

One guideline, albeit general, affects all investment adviser law. It is well established that investment advisers are fiduciaries and, as such, are held to a higher standard of care in their dealings with clients.[47] Furthermore, it is established that financial planners, in most cases, are investment advisers, and thus fiduciaries, for purposes of the Act.[48]

Few topics evoke as much heated discussion as the fiduciary issue. However, both the courts and the regulators have consistently adopted this position.[49] Consequently, investment advisers need to be sensitive to the fact that the courts and the regulators will generally construe the applicable securities laws and regulations liberally to protect the public unless there is clearly no investment adviser error. The position of the courts and the regulators is that Congress intended the Investment Advisers Act to be construed like other securities legislation "enacted for the purpose of avoiding frauds," not technically and restrictively, but flexibly to effectuate its remedial purposes.[50]

The investment adviser's duty to only recommend prudent investments is essentially absolute and rests solely on the investment adviser. Investment advisers have asserted a number of defenses in an attempt to avoid liability for imprudent investment advice. The courts and the regulators have generally rejected such defenses and, in so doing, have established a number of useful guidelines for investment advisers. In rejecting such defenses, the courts and the regulators have held that

- a client's opinion as to the prudence of an investment adviser's investment advice is irrelevant in the determination of prudence;[51]
- a client's ability to bear investment losses is irrelevant in the determination of prudence;[52]
- an investment adviser's honest, good faith belief that their investment advice was prudent is irrelevant in the determination of prudence;[53]
- imprudent investment advice is not made prudent simply because it results in a profit for a client;[54]
- the fact that a client's overall portfolio shows a profit does not insulate an investment adviser from liability for imprudent investment advice;[55]
- an investment adviser's reliance on a compliance officer's opinion on prudence does not prevent the imposition of liability for imprudent investment advice;[56]
- an investment adviser's ignorance of their business does not prevent the imposition of liability for imprudent investment advice;[57]
- a client's failure or refusal to provide personal information does not prevent the imposition of liability for imprudent investment advice;[58]
- specific intent is not required to impose liability on an investment adviser for imprudent investment advice;[59]
- a client's oral consent to a proposed trading strategy does not change the client's indicated investment objectives, risk tolerance level, or other personal investment parameters;[60]
- a client's level of sophistication does not necessarily indicate a client's knowledge or understanding of investing terms and concepts;[61]
- an investment adviser has a duty to prevent a client from committing "financial suicide."[62]

While most of these prudence decisions technically involved brokers, it is logical to assume that, given the purpose and intent of the Act, the same reasoning would be applied to all investment advisers.

Once imprudence has been determined, the only question left to be answered in determining whether an investment adviser is liable for imprudent investment advice is whether the investment adviser "recommended "the investment to the client. Here again, in order to carry out the intent and purpose of the Act, "recommend" is given a very liberal interpretation to include just about any act informing the client about the existence of the investment. In fact, sanctions for prudence violations have even been imposed in some recent cases involving the execution of purely unsolicited orders.[63]

The significance of the investment adviser's designation as a fiduciary cannot be overemphasized due to the inherent liability implications. Consequently, the need for some sort of direction on objective prudence guidelines becomes even more important.

Chapter 6

Common Fiduciary Prudence Errors

Prudence is a difficult concept for many investment advisers to truly grasp due to the amount of subjectivity often involved. As a result, allegations of imprudent investment advice and breach of fiduciary duties are the leading bases for investor complaints, often accounting for approximately 95% of investor complaints annually.[64] Some of the common bases for breach of fiduciary duty of prudence claims include

- recommending investments that exceed the client's risk tolerance level;
- recommending investments that are inconsistent with a client's investment objectives, investment time horizon, age, financial needs (e.g., liquidity, income) or other personal investment parameters;
- failing to adequately comprehend and/or explain all investment's risks;
- understating an investment's risk and/or overstating an investment's expected return;
- recommending investments that fail to properly diversify a client's portfolio;
- recommending investments that are inconsistent with the investment adviser's original asset allocation recommendations and representations;
- recommending primarily non-income or low income producing investments to clients with a need for income,
- recommending primarily growth or aggressive growth investments to elderly clients, widows and inexperienced investors;
- recommending the purchase of annuities, especially variable annuities, inside an IRA or similar retirement accounts or to clients needing income or liquidity;
- recommending investments that are perennial laggards or that lack enough of a track record to allow for meaningful analysis;

- recommending inappropriate classes of mutual fund shares;
- recommending reallocation strategies where the costs of reallocation (e.g., fees, expenses, taxes) outweigh the alleged benefits of reallocation.

This list is by no means all-inclusive. As mentioned earlier, the courts and the regulators have a tremendous amount of flexibility under the Act to address and sanction any conduct that they feel needs to be addressed in order to protect the public.

The bases listed above are errors that commonly occur in connection with asset allocation activities and one, implementation errors, that is the foundation of a developing theory of imprudence liability that may entrap many advisers. Most of the bases mentioned above are self-explanatory and the recommendation-implementation gap problem has already been discussed. The risk tolerance issue and the personal investment parameters issue, however, are often misunderstood and merit further discussion.

Risk Tolerance

If you were to ask most investment advisers how to determine a client's risk tolerance level, they would probably say that you look at the client's answers to a risk tolerance questionnaire and/or the client answers to the risk tolerance and investment objectives sections on the brokerage account application. Investment advisers would most likely answer in this manner because they sincerely believe, and most likely have been taught, that those are acceptable methods for assessing a client's risk tolerance level.

Unfortunately, investment advisers who limit their risk tolerance assessment to these two methods increase the likelihood of providing imprudent investment advice to their clients. The courts and the regulators have consistently applied a two-prong risk tolerance test in assessing the prudence of an investment adviser's investment recommendations.[65] Investment advisers who fail to meet either prong of the test will be deemed to have violated the risk tolerance suitability requirements.

The first prong of the risk tolerance suitability test is to determine a client's willingness to assume investment risk. The most commonly used means of obtaining a client's willingness to accept investment risk is though the client's responses to the risk tolerance and investment objectives sections typically found on brokerage applications/new account forms and/or some form of risk tolerance questionnaire.

With regard to prudence issues, the courts and the regulators simply do not give brokerage applications and risk tolerance questionnaires much weight due to the average investor's inability to understand the terminology used in such forms and the difficulty in accurately answering such questions. Risk tolerance questionnaires that ask clients how much money the client would be comfortable losing do little to create respect with the courts and the regulators. Furthermore, studies have shown that investors often overstate their tolerance for risk due to their lack of adequate investment experience to accurately assess their true risk tolerance level.[66]

With regard to risk tolerance questionnaires, the courts and the regulators also realize that the results from such forms are highly questionable given the ability to influence the results by virtue of the questions asked/not asked, the way the questions are phrased, and both the number and weighting of the questions.

A common mistake with regard to risk tolerance questionnaires is to ignore other information that a client has provided, information that may invalidate the results of a risk tolerance questionnaire. An example of this would be a client who has indicated on their brokerage application that they have little or no tolerance for risk and/or that their primary investment objective is preservation of capital. In such circumstance, there is absolutely no need to ask a client to fill out a risk tolerance questionnaire, as the client's investment parameters have already been established.

Another common mistake with regard to the failure to coordinate the client's questionnaire responses with other available information involves the income oriented client whose portfolio consists entirely or primarily of conservative, income producing investments. The client is usually given a questionnaire that includes questions regarding the client's need for income. The client accurately indicates that their income needs are being met, which they are as a result of the income from the client's existing investment portfolio.

The risk tolerance questionnaire, however, has no way of knowing that the client's response is based on the income from the client's existing portfolio. Consequently, the risk tolerance questionnaire may assign the client a risk tolerance level that is inappropriate for the client and the software program, relying on the inappropriate risk tolerance assessment, may create asset allocation recommendations that are completely imprudent for the client. End result, imprudent investment advice for the client and indefensible liability for the investment adviser.

Software programs and risk tolerance questionnaires can be valuable tools for an investment adviser, but the investment adviser must recognize such tools for what they are, tools, nothing more than a beginning point. Investment advisers who want to reduce their chances of liability exposure for imprudent investment advice must go beyond blindly accepting the output from such tools at face value and must learn to properly interpret and coordinate such information in light of all of the available information.

Investment advisers must then take their interpretations of such information and properly factor in additional client information (e.g., the client's age, marital status, dependents, employment status allow the investment adviser to satisfy the second prong of the risk tolerance equation determining a client's ability to bear investment risk. It is the failure to properly satisfy this second prong that often results in an investment adviser exceeding a client's risk tolerance level.

A client's lack of investment experience and lack of familiarity with investment terms/concepts often results in a client overstating their risk tolerance level. In order to ensure that investors are adequately protected, the courts and the regulators have held that an investment adviser has a duty to determine a client's actual ability to bear risk.

In imposing this additional obligation on investment advisers, the courts and the regulators have apparently reasoned that given an investment adviser's experience and expertise, an investment adviser can help ensure that investors are not taken advantage of because of their lack of investment experience and/or their lack of understanding of investment terms and concepts. As the court ruled in determining to impose a fiduciary standard on a broker,

> [t]he touchstone is whether or not the customer has the intelligence and understanding to evaluate the broker's recommendations and to reject one when he thinks it unsuitable.[67]

> the issue is whether or not the customer, based on the information available to him and his ability to interpret it, can independently evaluate his broker's suggestions.[68]

This second prong of the risk tolerance equation has led to the development of the "financial suicide" theory of liability for imprudence. Perhaps the best known case involving "financial suicide" liability is the case of Peterzell v. Charles Schwab & Co.[69] ("Schwab"), where Schwab was held liable for a customer's unsolicited trading. While the FINRA acknowledged that the customer's trades were unsolicited, liability was still found based on the theory that Schwab had enough information to realize that the customer's ongoing pattern of trading was imprudent.

While the Schwab decision has been criticized by many in both the investment and the legal communities, it should serve as an example of just how seriously the courts and the regulators consider the investment adviser's risk tolerance assessment responsibilities. Investment advisers that do not properly address both prongs of the risk tolerance prudence test risk the imposition of substantial monetary fines and monetary damages. So how does an investment adviser satisfy both prongs of the risk tolerance prudence test? The client's answers to questions on brokerage applications, risk tolerance questionnaires and similar account documents are an acceptable starting point in assessing the client's willingness to assume investment risk.

As an investment adviser reviews a client's responses, they should be alert to any inconsistencies or other potential liability traps in the client's answers. Such inconsistencies should serve as possible red flags that a client may not understand the forms or may not be able to determine their personal investment parameters.

In either case, the Prudent Investment Adviser™ will resolve any inconsistencies and uncertainty by talking to the client prior to making any investment recommendations. An investment adviser who fails to do so, who decides to guess as to what the client's feelings are, will find themselves in an indefensible position in the event that prudence issues arise.[70]

Investment advisers should also be aware that there are clients who will deliberately enter inconsistent information, hoping that the investment adviser will overlook or ignore the inconsistencies so that the client will have a claim in the event that they suffer investment losses. Evidence that clients will engage in such acts can be seen in the Schwab case, where the customer had previously won a case against another broker-dealer for allowing him to engage in the same pattern of trading.[71]

Given the inherent bias of MPT based asset allocation software programs, asset allocation recommendations generated from such software programs are generally going to favor growth and aggressive growth oriented equity investments unless the investment adviser properly constrains the software program regarding a client's specific needs.

Certain situations are almost always certain to raise red flags with regard to risk tolerance, among them recommending equity investments to clients who have indicated that they (1) have little or no tolerance for risk, (2) have limited or no prior investing experience, (3) have a short investment time horizon, (4) are only interested in preservation of capital and/or income as investment objectives, and/or (5) have a financial need for income or conservative investments.

Proponents of this position claim that the risks and the volatility of any investment will be smoothed out over the longer period of time. The problem with this position is that it reflects a MPT approach to asset allocation that, as mentioned earlier, is not the applicable standard used by the courts and the regulators in assessing the legal prudence of investment advice.

While not the sole or primary determinant of prudence, a client's investment time horizon is usually an important factor in the asset allocation process. Recommendations to purchase equity investments or to follow a growth or an aggressive growth investment strategy would be imprudent unless the client had a long term investment horizon.

On the other hand, the client's investment time horizon would be basically irrelevant for investors with little or no tolerance for risk; with investment objectives of preservation of capital or current income; or whose age, employment status, or financial situation suggests a conservative investment strategy. A common example of the latter situation would be where investment advisers provide retirees with MPT based asset allocation recommendations on 401k and IRA rollovers. In many cases, the retiree's financial needs and overall financial situation will result in such recommendations being imprudent for the retiree, both practically and under the legal prudence standard.

An investment parameter often overlooked or undervalued is an investor's age.[72] Young investors may lack the experience or knowledge to understand and appreciate the concept of investment risk. Age alone, however, does not automatically equate to investment knowledge or sophistication.

Older clients maybe unable to understand or appreciate the risks of certain investments or investment strategies due to a limited amount or a complete lack of investment experience. The classic example is the investor whose only investment experience has been in ultra-safe fixed income investments such as certificates of deposit and treasuries. Investment adviser recommending a growth or an aggressive growth strategy in such cases may well increase their prudence liability exposure.

Age may also be relevant in any prudence analysis due to its potential impact on a client's ability to bear investment risk and to recover investment losses. For example, in most cases, the recommendation of aggressive growth investments or even an over-concentration in growth oriented investments to older clients would be highly suspect regardless of the client's indicated risk tolerance level, investment objectives or investment time horizon due to the potential financial impact of any losses and loss recovery time issues.

These are just two examples of the importance of considering all of a client's investment parameters before making investment recommendations. Liability for imprudent investment advice often results from an investment adviser's fixation on one or two of a client's investment parameters, often the client's investment time horizon and/or the client's net worth. The investment time horizon argument has already been discussed. Furthermore, the fact that a client's net worth may put the client in a better position to bear investment losses is totally irrelevant in assessing the prudence of investment advice.[73]

Chapter 7

Looking Forward

No one can predict the future. However, given the recent trend of increased market volatility and the continuing stories of alleged corporate and investment misconduct, it is probably safe to say that investment advisers will face increased scrutiny in the years to come.

Investment advisers can expect to see the courts and the regulators continue to act to provide greater protection for the public against questionable investment practices. The evolving nature of the concept of a Prudent Investment Adviser Rule™ will present challenges for investment advisers in order to stay in compliance with applicable legal and industry standards and to provide clients with quality investment advice.

Fiduciary Litigation

Two 2015 decisions may provide an indication that the trend of increased litigation over alleged breaches of fiduciary duties and investor protection will continue. Since these cases involve past actions that cannot be undone, the trend of multi-million dollar settlements and verdicts will likely continue as well.

In Tibble v. Edison International [74], the Supreme Court ruled that pension plan sponsors had on ongoing duty to monitor investment options within their plan and to remove options that were no longer prudent for the plan. The plan had tried to argue that after six years, the general statute of limitation for actions under ERISA, a plan participant or beneficiary could not bring an action based on the plan's investment options.

The Court ruled that the applicable six-year statute of limitations began anew with each review of the investment options by the plan's sponsor or other investment fiduciary. The ruling definitely increase the likelihood that plan participants and beneficiaries will pursue their legal rights against plans as they learn more about investing and the proper evaluation of investment options within their plan.

In <u>Leber v. The Citigroup 401k Plan Investment Committee</u>[75], a decision on a preliminary motion for summary judgment should definitely have potential long-term implications for both ERISA and non-ERISA fiduci aries. The action involves allegations of excessive fees in connection with a 401k plan.

The court actually handed down two important rulings. In the first ruling, the court ruled that the Vanguard family of funds were acceptable for the purposes of comparing fees among available investment options. Given the fact that Vanguard's fees are generally among the lowest in the mutu al fund industry, this definitely imposes a greater challenge on plan spon sors to justify the choice of more expensive, and often underperforming, actively managed investment options for their plans.

Secondly, the court addressed ERISA three-year statute of limitations when plan participants have actual knowledge of the plan sponsor's breach of their fiduciary duties or other violations of ERISA. The court ruled that the actual knowledge requirement must be strictly construed. Consequently, what plan participants and beneficiaries "should have known" or what they suspected was insufficient to meet the "actual knowledge of all the facts material to their claim" required of the three-year statute of limitations statute.

While the court's decision is not technically binding on other courts, the court's reasoning makes it more likely than not that other courts will adopt the court's position. The court's ruling that "what matters are the facts plaintiffs possess, not the facts they suspect or could discover" pro vides plan participants and beneficiaries with a potentially powerful ar gument in future litigations.

Investment advisers looking for another sign as to the future of liability for imprudent investment advice may want to examine a recent case in which the investors' allegations of imprudence were based, in part, on the existence of recommendation-implementation gaps.[76] The investors sued the individual financial adviser and his company for losses incurred in connection with investments recommended and sold to them by the investment adviser, citing the inconsistency between the recommendations and the investment adviser's specific investment recommendations.

The case is significant for investment advisers due to the court's ruling that questions regarding the prudence of investment advice and an investment adviser's fiduciary duties are questions of fact that must be determined by a jury or other trier of fact. The investment adviser and his company had asked the court to dismiss the case on the grounds that the plaintiffs had been given prospectuses for the investments in question and that the prospectuses clearly indicated the risks involved with the investments. The court rejected such arguments, ruling that the fiduciary nature of a investment adviser-client relationship creates questions of fact regarding a fiduciary's duties that the court cannot properly determine.

The investors' allegations of liability based on recommendation-implementation gaps represent the development of a new theory of investment adviser prudence liability. Given the fact that many investment advisers cannot or do not perform a post-implementation check for recommendation-implementation gaps, the court's ruling is especially significant due to the precedent it sets. The court's ruling also sends a clear message that the courts and the regulators will continue to hold investment advisers and other fiduciaries to a higher standard of care in order to protect the public.

Closely connected to the recommendation-implementation gaps issue is the issue of investment style, particularly the issues of style only investing and "style drift." Style only investing refers to the assumption that any investment is suitable in implementing asset allocation recommendations as long as the investment chosen falls within the applicable asset category. While this assumption is consistent with the assumptions used in MPT, it is not consistent with the legal suitability standard.

To satisfy the legal fiduciary prudence standard, an investment adviser needs to analyze both the style and substance of any investment products recommended. The investment adviser's first step should be to invest "by style," to diversify across asset categories, or styles, making sure that the investments chosen are consistent with the original asset allocation recommendations, both as to style and amount.

The second step should be to invest "by substance," to choose specific investments that ensure that the portfolio actually implemented is consistent with the assumptions used in producing the original asset allocation recommendations and the original risk and return projections for the recommended portfolio. Failure to perform either of these steps may result in recommendation-implementation gaps and liability exposure for the investment adviser.

Style drift may become an issue in performing both steps. Style drift refers to situations where some mutual funds or other investments drift from one investment style, or orientation, to a different style. Style drift can have a significant effect on a client's asset allocation, and thus the risk and return characteristics of the client's overall portfolio.

A prime example of the significance of style drift can be seen in the changes that occurred when Jeff Vinick took over as manager of the Fidelity Magellan mutual fund. Under Peter Lynch, Magellan was generally considered a fairly diversified equity growth fund. When Vinick took over, one of his early moves was to make significant sector plays. Later on, he created quite a stir in the investment community when he allocated a significant amount of the fund's assets to bonds. Vinick's tenure as Magellan's portfolio manager was short lived, as his strategic moves resulted in substandard performance.

The potential for style drift will require investment advisers to perform more research prior to recommending specific investments for implementation of their asset allocation recommendations. Investment advisers who blindly accept the representations contained in prospectuses without reviewing current information on the investment product may be held liable for failing to perform the due diligence necessary to produce the reasonable basis required for any investment recommendation.[77] The Prudent Investment Adviser™ will determine whether the investment has shown style drift tendencies and assess the investment's recent and historical performance.

In light of ongoing issues on Wall Street, it can also be assumed that both the courts and the regulators will require investment advisers to provide more disclosure, both in terms of quantity and quality. The courts and the regulators have already held that the investment adviser's duty of disclosure requires more than simply providing a client with a prospectus.

Investment advisers must explain an investment's risks to a client in such a way that the client clearly understands such risks.[78] Disclosure must also be complete and meaningful, providing the client with all material information about an investment.[79] In the words of one court, the law "provides no protection to someone who warns his hiking companion to walk slowly because there might be a ditch ahead when he knows with near certainty that the Grand Canyon lies one foot away."[80]

To sum up, both ERISA and non-ERISA investment fiduciaries can expect to see fiduciary based litigation continue, if not increase as more people more informed about their rights and the extent of breaches of fiduciary duties by investment fiduciaries. Furthermore, investment fiduciaries can expect to see more fiduciary based litigation by not only clients and/or plan participants, but also by heirs, ex-spouses and divorcing spouses who realize that they have derivative rights to bring such actions. The prudent investment fiduciary will be proactive in limiting potential liability exposure.

Fiduciary "Red Flag" Products

Variable Annuities
Certain investments have proven to consistently raise red flags for investment advisers and other investment fiduciaries. Variable annuities consistently rank among the leading source of investors complaints with regulators.

The variable annuity industry has consistently tried to convince investment advisers to recommend the product. However, prudent investment advisers and other fiduciaries know that several aspects of most variable annuities, most notably the high fees assessed by variable annuities and the inequitable methods used in calculating such fees, guarantee that variable annuities will never pass the fiduciary standard's basic "best interests" test.

Fees and Others Costs of Variable Annuities
The costs associated with variable annuities and the method of calculating such costs are primary reasons for the variable annuities failing the fiduciary "best interests" test. Most variable annuity issuers calculate their annual fees using a method known as "inverse pricing," a method calculates a variable annuity's annual fees based on the accumulated value of the investments within the variable annuity.

Since most variable annuities limit the amount payable under the annuity's death benefit to the actual amount of the annuity owner's actual contribution to the annuity, inverse pricing guarantees a windfall for the annuity issuer even if they have to pay the variable annuity's heirs when the owner dies. That windfall is even greater, as the seminal study by Moshe Milevsky concluded that the fee charged for the variable annuity's death benefit feature is often ten times greater than its actual value. [81] Again, prudent investment advisers do not recommend variable annuities.

The total annual fee charged on most variable annuities is approximately 2 percent of the overall value of the variable annuity. Add the management fee, often in the range of an additional 1 percent for the subaccounts within the variable annuity and it is not unusual to see total fees in the range of 3 percent. Given the fact that each additional 1 percent in investment fees reduces an investor's end return by approximately 17 percent over a twenty year period…smart, prudent fiduciaries avoid variable annuities.

Quality of Variable Annuity Investment Options

Another fiduciary issue with variable annuities is the fact that an investor's investment options within the variable annuity are determined by the variable annuity issuer, not the investor. It is not uncommon to see investment options within a variable annuity with the deadly combination of high fees and less than stellar performance records. Even worse, in many cases this combination is due to variable annuity issuers filling their variable annuities with their proprietary products of those of an affiliated company. Investment adviser can use the Active Management Value Ratio™ to quickly evaluate the investment options within an annuity.

In short, in most cases variable annuities are a breach of fiduciary duty just waiting to happen. A detailed analysis of variable annuities and some of the marketing strategies used to sell them are set out in Appendix E.

Equity Indexed Annuities

Technically, EIAs are not an investment product, but they are an insurance-based fixed income annuity that bases it annual return on the performance of an investment index rather than a predetermined rate of return. Since investment advisers, often obtain an insurance license as well as a securities license, this discussion is intended to alert investment advisers to potential liability issues.

These products go by various names. The key feature of indexed annuities (EIAs) is that the return they provide is tied to some investment index, such as the S&P 500 or the DJIA. At least that what most investors believe based on the marketing strategies often used in connection with these products. Investors see the double digit returns often posted by the S&P 500 and decide to purchase an EIA. However, that is one of the fiduciary prudence issues presented by EIAs, as some might say that the marketing of equity indexed annuities can mislead the public due to the severe restrictions placed on the indexed annuity owner's ability to fully participate in an index's gain.

Most equity-indexed annuities limit, or "cap," the owner's annual gain to 10-12% regardless of the index's actual gain. The owner's ability to participate in the index's gain is further restricted by the imposition of a "par ticipation rate," typically in the range of 70-80 percent. For example, if an investor owned an EIA that capped the annuity owner's gain at 10 per cent, with a participation rate of 70 percent, the most that the annuity owner could earn for that year would be 7 percent (10 percent x .70), even if the index actually gained 30 percent that year.

Some EIAs do offer downside protection by guaranteeing a minimum annual return for yet another fee. Nevertheless, when an investor in an index based product is limited to a gain of 7 percent when the index itself shows a much larger gain, it is easy to understand why EIAs present potential fiduciary "best interest" liability concerns.

A good general rule of thumb for investment advisers and other investment fiduciaries is that any product that imposes "caps" or otherwise limits a client's return should immediately raise potential red flags and the adviser or fiduciary should conduct a detailed analysis of the product and ensure proper and adequate disclosure to a client.

Proprietary Mutual Funds

The two primary issues presented by proprietary mutual funds are costs and performance. From a fiduciary and liability perspective, proprietary funds often have high fees and/or poor performance records. Dually registered investment advisers are often pressured to sell investment products of their broker-dealer, with generous rewards for doing so.

Some investment advisors and other investment fiduciaries attempt to justify recommending imprudent proprietary mutual funds under a rational known as the "two hats" theory. The two hats theory claims that a dually registered investment adviser only owes a customer a fiduciary duty when the adviser is providing investment advice as an investment adviser, but not when the adviser is acting as a broker and recommending and selling actual investment products.

The two hats theory developed in connection with ERISA, where there is a clear difference between acting in an administrative capacity and an investment fiduciary. The courts have clearly rejected the two hats argument in connection with dually registered brokers, stating that

> The record shows clearly that, except for a few isolated instances, petitioner acted simultaneously in the dual capacity of investment adviser and of broker and dealer. In such capacity, conflicting interests must necessarily arise. When they arise, the law has consistently stepped in to provide safeguards in the form of prescribed and stringent standards of conduct on the part of the fiduciary. More than 100 years ago the Supreme Court set forth this principle as follows:

> In this conflict of interest, the law wisely interposes. It acts not on the possibility, that, in some cases, the sense of that duty may prevail over the motives of self-interest, but it provides against the probability in many cases, and the danger in all cases, that the dictates of self-interest will exercise a predominant influence, and supersede that of duty.[82]

Leveraged and Inverse Mutual Funds

Greed raises its ugly head when talk of leveraged and/or inverse mutual funds arises. From a fiduciary standpoint, the increased risk associated with such products will make them imprudent for most investors and fiduciaries. Even if an investor raises the subject unsolicited, the prudent investment adviser should strongly consider refusing to participate in the purchase of these products to ensure that potential breach of fiduciary duty allegations are totally avoided.

Inverse index mutual funds are used by some investment advisers to hedge against significant portfolio losses. While simple inverse funds can be successfully used for such purposes, it is crucial that an investment contemplating such as strategy totally understand how these products work.

While the returns of unleveraged inverse funds may be 100 percent negatively correlated to the underlying index, there is no guarantee that that correlation will always remain consistent. A safer strategy for investment advisers and other investment fiduciaries may be to use protective puts to protect a client's portfolio against significant losses.

A number of mutual fund companies offer inverse mutual funds with various levels of leverage. It simply is not worth the risk for an investment adviser or investment fiduciary to recommend or participate in any dealings with these products. Even if a client's risk tolerance profile suggests that these products are acceptable, these products are so susceptible to quick and significant losses that the prudent investment adviser will avoid any involvement with them. Furthermore, these are easy targets for investor plaintiff attorneys, as given the unusual nature of these products, it is easy to claim that investor did not fully understand the risk involved and/or that the investment adviser did not properly explain the product or its risk.

Unauthorized Trading

Investment fiduciaries that manage client accounts on a discretionary basis often do so by relying solely on a document known in the industry as a "trading authorization." What many investment fiduciaries donot know is that while a trading authorization is accepted in the industry, a trading authorization alone is not legally sufficient to empower a investment fiduciary to trade in and on behalf of a client account. Therefore, investment fiduciaries that rely solely on a trading authorization leave themselves exposed to a claim of unauthorized trading.

Legally, the proper document that authorizes one person to act on behalf of another is known as a power of attorney. Investment fiduciaries should have a client execute a limited power of attorney authorizing the investment fiduciary to place trades and otherwise manage the client's investment account(s) on a discretionary basis.

Investment fiduciaries that use custodians for their clients' accounts are often required to enter into some sort of master agreement with the custodian. What investment fiduciaries often do not realize is that somewhere in the master agreement in language stating that the investment fiduciary agrees to obtain all documents legally required in to manage their clients' accounts on a discretionary basis.

The agreement typically goes on to state that in the event the investment fiduciary does not obtain all such legally required documents, then the investment fiduciary agree to hold the custodian harmless and to reimburse the custodian for any and all damages imposed against the custodian for the investment fiduciary's failure to obtain such required documents. Given the high costs of litigation, as well as possible fines and reimbursement of any losses and trading costs incurred by an account, investment fiduciaries need to carefully read their master agreements with any custodians they use in connection with clients' accounts and ensure that they are in full compliance with the terms of such custodial agreements.

Chapter 8

Final Exam

Time to pull together the major points that have been presented and analyze an actual issue that is gaining more attention and one that most investment advisers will deal with more than once during their career, one that has already been raised in fiduciary litigation and one with definite potential breach of fiduciary duty implications.

As mentioned earlier, one of a fiduciary's primary duties is the duty of loyalty. The Restatement (Third) Trusts states that the fiduciary duty of loyalty requires that

> Whether acting in a fiduciary or personal capacity, a [fiduciary] has a duty in dealing with a [client] to deal fairly and to communicate to the [client] all material facts the [fiduciary] knows or should know in connection with the [account].[83]

Therefore, a fiduciary has a legal duty to disclose all "material" facts to a client. The next question is obviously what constitutes a "material fact?" The most common definition of a material fact is

> whether a [client] would consider the information important in making an investment decision.[84]

The emerging issue for investment advisers and other investment fiduciaries involves the common situation where an investment adviser obtains a new client and reviews the current assets in the client's investment portfolio. As a former compliance director, I am well aware that the common practice is to recommend replacing all or most of the current portfolio's investments and replacing them new funds, thereby generating compensation for the financial/investment adviser.

Since it is illegal to recommend replacing a client's current investments for the sole purpose of generating compensation for the financial/ investment adviser, we will assume that the recommendation to replace any of a client's current investment was based on the "best interests" of a client.

If that were not the case, the client may have a legal claim against a former financial/investment adviser for recommending unsuitable and imprudent investments, especially if the investor to suffer any financial loss. Most people would definitely consider such information to be "material."

When this scenario and the question of the fiduciary's duty to disclose such information is brought up, most financial/ investment advisers quickly claim that they have no duty to disclose such information since they are not attorneys and therefore cannot accurately interpret whether securities laws and regulations have been violated. They also point out that they could face liability themselves if they falsely accuse another financial/ investment adviser of acting illegally.

A good securities attorney is going to counter with the point that financial/investment advisers have a duty to evaluate any products that they recommend, so they know, or should know, how to evaluate the prudence of an investment for a particular client. With regard to mutual funds, the Active Management Value Ratio™ provides a simple and effective method of evaluating both their own recommendations as well as the recommendations of any other investment professional.

As far as the issue of creating potential personal liability for suggesting that another investment professional has acted improperly, a good attorney is going to counter that a general suggestion to a client that they may want to consult a securities attorney should not result in any liability exposure, especially if the suggestion is being made pursuant to an adviser's fiduciary duty of disclosure and loyalty.

In many cases, a complicating factor is whether the adviser is dually registered with both a broker-dealer's brokerage unit and their proprietary investment advisory firm. A broker-dealer is generally not going to allow one of their brokers to accuse another broker of illegal activity, regardless of whether it is one of their own brokers or a broker for another broker-dealer.

If an adviser is dually registered, but they are register with an independent investment advisory firm, the adviser is faced with a totally different issue since legally a broker-dealer's only legal duties and responsibilities with regard to brokers affiliated with independent investment advisory firms is to supervise the broker's securities trading activity. However, it would be naïve to think that a broker is not going to consider instructions from their broker-dealer, even if the broker-dealer has no legal right to dictate their activity within an investment advisory firm.

So, what does an investment adviser or other investment fiduciary do in such a situation? The Restatement (Second) of Trusts § 223 addresses the liability of a successor trustee (fiduciary) stating that

> (1) A trustee is not liable to the beneficiary for breach of trust
> (2) A trustee is liable to the beneficiary for breach of trust, if he
> (a) knows or should know of a situation constituting a breach of trust committed by his predecessor and he improperly permits it to continue; or...
> (c) neglects to take proper steps to redress a breach of trust committed by the predecessor.[85]

The Restatement generally requires an investment adviser to sue a predecessor investment adviser or other investment fiduciary for actual or questionable activity during their management of an account. An argument can be made that a more prudent course of business would be for an investment adviser to alert their client to a potential breach of fiduciary duty by the predecessor fiduciary and then allow the client to follow through with an attorney should they wish to do so, with either the client or the fiduciary bringing an action based on the attorney's advice.

Again, this is an emerging issue and one that is not uncommon. I regularly get calls from advisers and fiduciaries that have either read something that I wrote on this issue or have heard me speak on same.

This is analogous to the estate planning recommendation on having a will prepared–regardless what a client decides, to prepare a will or not, an estate plan is going to be created. The only issue is whether the client or Uncle Sam determines the disposition of the client's property. The key for investment advisers and other investment fiduciaries is to be aware of such issues in order to properly evaluate and manage potential professional liability situations.

Chapter 9

Summary

Prudence can be a somewhat elusive concept to grasp, but it is one that investment advisers must understand in order to avoid the various asset allocation prudence traps that confront them. A large part of avoiding fiduciary prudence traps involves an investment adviser's understanding of

- the asset allocation process, particularly with regard to MPT;
- the inherent weaknesses and biases of asset allocation software programs; especially those based on MPT, also known as means-variance optimization; and
- the difference between theoretical prudence and legal prudence under the "prudent man" standard as set out in the Restatement (Third) Trusts' Prudent Investor Rule.

Investment advisers can get so caught up with asset allocation theories and software programs that they fail to properly provide for their client's needs and objectives, resulting in imprudent investment advice for the client and unnecessary liability exposure for the investment adviser.

In the rush to gather assets to manage, some investment advisers fail to take the time to learn the applicable legal and regulatory standards by which their investment advisory activities will be evaluated. Prudent investment advisers who do take the time to learn such standards will learn that with regard to the prudence of investment advice, legal reality takes priority over financial/ economic theory. Investment advice that fails to pass the applicable legal prudence standards will generally result in liability for the investment adviser, regardless of which financial theory or technique the investment adviser used in producing such advice.

In expectation of an even greater pro-investor stance by the courts and the regulators, today's investment fiduciaries must become more proactive and assume greater responsibility for ensuring that their activities are in compliance with all applicable legal standards. Ignoring the applicable law and legal developments in the investment industry is clearly not a prudent course of action. As Abraham Lincoln said, "[y]ou can't escape the responsibility of tomorrow by evading it today."

Investment advisers who believe that liability for imprudent investment advice can be avoided by simply claiming ignorance of such standards or that the investment adviser acted in good faith should heed the admonition that "a pure heart and an empty head"[86] is not an acceptable defense to breach of fiduciary duty claims.

The Prudent Investment Adviser Rule™ is a living concept that will adapt over time to reflect changes in applicable laws as well as future legal decisions. The Prudent Investment Adviser Rule™ will hopefully help investment advisers better understand some of the applicable standards regarding the prudence of their investment advice and avoid some of the common asset allocation prudence traps, thereby allowing investment advisers to better serve their clients and to protect their practices.

Notes

1. Securities and Exchange Commission v. Capital Gains Research Bureau, 375 U.S. 180, 194 (1963)

2. Howard v. Shay, 100 F.3d 1484, 1488 (9th Cir. 1996); Donovan v. Bierwirth, 680 F.2d 263, 272 n. 8 (2d Cir. 1982)

3. Meinhard v. Salmon, 249 N.Y. 458, 464 (1928)

4. Leigh v. Engle, 727 F.2d 113, 125-27 (7th Cir. 1984)

5. Restatement (Third) Trusts § 90

6. Investment Advisers Act of 1940, 15 U.S.C. §§ 80b-1 et seq.

7. *See*, e.g., In re George Sein Lin, 43 S.E.C. Docket 1840, 1841 (1989)

8. Investment Advisers Act of 1940, § 80b-6, Rule 206, 17 C.F.R. § 275.206.

9. Securities and Exchange Act of 1934 (Exchange Act), 15 U.S.C. § 78j(b), Rule 10b-5, 17 C.F.R. § 240.10b-5.

10. Securities and Exchange Act of 1934 (Exchange Act), 15 U.S.C. § 78a-78jj, as amended.

11. *See*, e.g., Miley v. Oppenheimer & Co., 637 F.2d 318, 333 (5th Cir.), reh'g denied, 624 F.2d 1210 (5th Cir. 1981); Merrill Lynch, Pierce, Fenner & Smith, Inc. v. Cheng, 697 F. Supp. 1224, 1227 (D.C. Cir. 1988).

12. Investment Advisers Act Release No. 1406 ((March 16, 1994).

13. Harry M. Markowitz, *Portfolio Selection: Efficient Diversification of Investments*," 2nd Ed. (Cambridge, MA: Basil Blackwood & Sons, Inc., 1991); Harry M. Markowitz, "Portfolio Selection," *Journal of Finance*, March 1952.

14. William F. Sharpe, "Financial Planning in Fantasyland," available at www. stanford.edu/~wfsharpe/art/fantasy/ fantasy.htm.

15. Johnston v. CIGNA Securities, 916 P.2d 643, 647 (Colo. App. 1996).

16. William F. Sharpe, *"Investors and Market: Portfolio Choices, Asset Prices and Investment Advice,"* (Princeton University Press:Princteon, NJ 2006), 207-208.

17. See, e.g., Wedbush Securities, 40 S.E.C. Docket 710, 715 (1988): Larry Ira Klein, 63 S.E.C. Docket 52, 56 (1996); DeKwiatkowski v. Bear Stearns & Co., Inc., 126 F.2d 672, 690 (S.D.N.Y. 2000). Rule 10b-5,

supra, also establishes a transactional standard for review of assessing the prudence of investment advice.

18. Uniform Prudent Investor Act §§ 1-16, 7B U.L.A. 18.

19. Restatement (Third) Trusts § 227.

20. Exchange Act, *supra*.

21. *See, e.g.,* R. Michaud, *Efficient Asset Management,* (Boston, MA: Harvard Business School Press, 1998); R. Michaud, "The Markowitz Optimization Enigma: Is "Optimized" Optimal," *Financial Analysts Journal,* January/February 1989;

22. R. Campbell, K. Koedijk and P. Kofman, "Increased Correlation in Bear Markets," *Financial Analysts Journal,* January/ February 2002; E. Jacquier and A. Marcus, "Asset Allocation Models and Market Volatility," *Financial Analysts Journal,* March/April 2001.

23. Markowitz, 2nd ed., 6-7.

24. Markowitz, 2nd ed., 125.

25. *See*, e.g., William F. Sharpe, Gordon J. Alexander and Jeffery V. Bailey, "The Trouble with Optimizers," *Investments*, 5th ed. (Englewood Cliffs, NJ: Prentice Hall 1995); 198-199; Scott Lummer, Mark W. Riepe and Laurence B. Siegel, "Taming Your Optimizer: A Guide Through the Pitfalls of Mean-Variance Optimization," *Global Asset Allocation: Techniques for Optimizing Portfolio Management*," ed. Jess Lederman and Robert A. Klein, (New York: John Wiley and Sons 1994).

26. Michaud, *Efficient*, 36

27. Jacquier and Marcus, *supra*.

28. Sharpe, *Fantasyland, supra*.

29. SEC v. Capital Gains Research Bureau, Inc., 375 U.S. 180, 199-200, 11 L. Ed. 2d 237, 84 S. Ct. 275 (1963); Charles Hughes & Co. v. SEC, 139 F.2d 434, 437 (1943).

30. 17 C.F.R. § 240.10b-5

31. Uniform Prudent Investor Act §7, comment

32. Charles D. Ellis, *"Murder on the Orient Express,"* p.5

33. Burton Malkiel, *"A Random Walk Down Wall Street:The Time-Tested Strategy for Successful Investing,"* 12th ed. (W.W. Norton & Co., Inc: New York 2015), 401

34. *See*, e.g., FINRA Conduct Rule 2310, *supra*; Lin, *supra*, 1841; Paul F. Wickswat, 50 SEC Docket 165, 166 (1991).

35. Investment Advisers Act Release No. 58 (April 10, 1951); Investment Advisers Act of 1940 § 215, 15 U.S.C. § 80b-15, Rule 206, 17 C.F.R. § 275.215.

36. Erdos, 183; Wickswat, 166.

37. See. e.g., John M. Reynolds, Exchange Acr Rel. 34-30036, 50 S.E.C. Docket 504, 506-07 (12-4-1991); Clyde J. Bruff, 52 S.E.C. Docket 1266, 1268 (1992); Charles W. Eye, 49 S.E.C. Docket 851, 854 (1991).

38. Investment Advisers Act of 1940 §§ 206, 215, *supra.*

39. Markowitz, 2nd ed., *supra.*

40. Capital Gains, supra; Hughes v. SEC, 174 F.2d 969, 975 (D.C. Cir. 1949).

41. Restatement (Third) Trusts § 227.

42. Restatement (Third) Trusts § 227.

43. Restatement (Third) Trusts § 227.

44. "Redefining the 'Prudent Investor Rule' for Trustees," *Trusts and Estates*, (December 1990); Restatement (Third) Trusts § 227. "General Notes" on comments e through h.

45. Restatement (Third) Trusts § 227, "General Notes" on comments e through h.

46. Restatement (Third) Trusts § 227, comments d and e.

47. Investment Advisers Act Release No. 1092 (October 8, 1987); Capital Gains, *supra*, 194.

48. Investment Advisers Act Release No. 1092 (October 8, 1987); Johnston, *supra*, 647.

49. Capital Gains, *supra*, 247; Johnston, *supra*, 647.

50. Capital Gains, at 195.

51. Erdos, at 183; Wickswat, at 166.

52. Klein, at 57: Wedbush, at 715.

53. Clinton Hugh Holland, 60 S.E.C. Docket 2507, 2510 (1995); Capital Gains, at 251.

54. Erdos, at 182-183.

55. Klein, at 57; Wedbush, at 715.

56. Klein, at 57.

57. Thomas Arthur Smith, 20 S.E.C. Docket 196, 207 (1945).

58. Erdos, at 57; Hellie, at 638.

59. Erdos, at 57.

60. Wickswat, at 166.

61. Klein, at 55.

62. *See.* e.g., Peterzell v. Charles Schwab & Co., FINRA Arbitration 88-02868 1991 WL 202358 (June 17, 1991) (Townsend, Arb); Quick & Reilly, Inc. v. Barton, NYSE Case No. 90-2033, 1990 WL 306396 (February 15, 1990) (Shoemaker, Hall , Grigsby, Arbs.).

63. Schwab, *supra*.

64. *"ZARB Urges Broker Dealers to 'Be on Guard' About Prudence,"* 30 Sec. Reg. L. Rep. (BNA) No. 22, at 810 (may 29, 1998).

65. See, e.g., Klein, at 57; F.J. Kaufmann & Co. of Virginia, 45 S.E.C. Docket 97, 100 (1989); In re James B. Chase, FINRA Adjudicatory Council, available online at http://www.finra.org/sites/default/files/ NAC Decision/p007064.pdf

66. Solveig Jannson, "Is Preservation of Capital Making a Comeback?" 8 *Institutional Investor*, 55, 56-57 (April 1974).

67. Follansbee v. Davis, Skaggs & Co., Inc., 681 F.2d 673, 677 (9th Cir. 1982)

68. Carras v. Burns, 516 F.2d 251, 258 (4th Cir. 1975)

69. Schwab, *supra*.

70. Erdos, at 183; Hellie, at 637.

71. Peterzell v. Dean Witter Reynolds, Inc., American Arbitration Case No. 32-136-0416-88-10 (November 9, 1990).

72. Leib v. Merrill Lynch, Pierce, Fenner & Smith, Inc., 461 F. Supp. 951, 954 (D. Mich. 1978).

73. Klein, at 57; Hellie, at 637.

74. Tibble v. Edison International, 135 U.S. 1823, 1828 (2015)

75. Leber v. The Citigroup 401k Plan Investment Committee, Case No. 07-Cv-9329 (S.D.N. Y. 2014)

76. Johnston, *supra*

77. Chase, supra; Bruff, at 1267-1268; Johnston, at 648; In re Prudential Securities Incorporated Limited Partnership Litigation, 930 Supp. 68, 72 (S.D.N.Y 1996).

78. Chase, supra; Bruff, at 1268-1269.

79. Chase, supra; Prudential, at 72.

80. Prudential, at 72.

81. Moshe Milevsky and Steven Posner, "The Titanic Option: Valuation of the Guaranteed Death Benefit in Variable Annuities and Mutual Funds," *Journal of Risk and Insurance*, Vol. 68, No. 1, (2001), 91-126.

82. <u>Hughes v S.E.C.</u>, 174 F.2d 969, 975 (D.C.C. 1949)
83. Restatement (Third) Trusts §78
84<u>. S.E.C. v. Rogers</u>, 790 F.2d 1450, 1458 (9th Cir. 1986)
85. Restatement (Second) Trusts §223
86.<u>Donovan v. Cunningham</u>, 716 F.2d 1455, 1467 (5th Cir. 1983)

APPENDIX A

AMVR™ Worksheet

	Costs	Total Costs	Return
Actively Managed Fund			
Active ER			
Active T/O*			
Index Fund			
Index ER			
Index T/O*			
Incremental			
%			

70

AMVR™ Worksheet

	Costs	Total Costs	Return
Actively Managed Fund			10.00
Active ER	1.00		
Active T/O*	0.48	1.48	
Index Fund			9.00
Index ER	0.20		
Index T/O*	0.04.	0.24	
Incremental		1.24	1.00
%		91%	10%

*T/O Cost = [Stated turnover ratio x 2] x 0.60

Active fund not cost effective, so imprudent investment. Fund's incremental cost exceeds incremental return, and 91% of active fund's fee only producing 10% of fund's return. With index fund, investor can receive 90% of actively managed fund's return for only 20% of the actively managed fund's fee.

APPENDIX B

Restatement (Third) Trusts - § 227
General Standard of Prudent Investment

The trustee has a duty to the beneficiaries to invest and manage the funds of the trust as a prudent investor would, in light of the purposes, terms, distribution requirements, and other circumstances of the trust.

(a) This standard requires the exercise of reasonable care, skill, and caution, and is to be applied to investments not in isolation but in the context of the trust portfolio and as a part of an overall investment strategy, which should incorporate risk and return objectives reasonably suitable to the trust.

(b) In making and implementing investment decisions, the trustee has a duty to diversity the investments of the trust unless, under the circumstances, it is prudent not to do so.

(c) In addition, the trustee must:

(1) conform to fundamental fiduciary duties of loyalty (§ 78) and impartiality (§ 79);

(2) act with prudence in deciding whether and how to delegate authority and in the selection   and supervision of agents (§ 80); and

(3) incur only costs that are reasonable in amount and appropriate to the investment responsibilities of the trusteeship (§ 88).

APPENDIX C

29 U.S.C. § 1104: ERISA 404 - Fiduciary Liability

(a) Prudent man standard of care

(1) Subject to sections 1103(c) and (d), 1342, and 1344 of this title, a fiduciary shall discharge his duties with respect to a plan solely in the interest of the participants and beneficiaries and—

(A) for the exclusive purpose of: (i) providing benefits to participants and their beneficiaries; and (ii) defraying reasonable expenses of administering the plan;

(B) with the care, skill, prudence, and diligence under the circumstances then prevailing that a prudent man acting in a like capacity and familiar with such matters would use in the conduct of an enterprise of a like character and with like aims;

(C) by diversifying the investments of the plan so as to minimize the risk of large losses, unless under the circumstances it is clearly prudent not to do so; and

(D) in accordance with the documents and instruments governing the plan insofar as such documents and instruments are consistent with the provisions of this subchapter and subchapter III.

The Employee Retirement Income Security Act of 1974 (ERISA) is essentially a codification of the Restatement (Second) and (Third) of Trusts. As a result, both statutes have an obvious overlap in the four traditional fiduciary duties (loyalty, care, diversification of plan assets, and adherence to plan documents, where prudent.)

ERISA does have some additional requirements and clarifications, some of which evolved primarily due to regulatory and legal decisions and interpretations. The primary differences between the Restatement and ERISA are that ERISA imposes duties upon a broader class of fiduciaries, prohibits exculpatory clauses, has broad disclosure and reporting requirements, and requires nationwide uniformity of rules.

While a complete and detailed discussion of ERISA's fiduciary rules and regulations are beyond the scope of this book, a brief reference to ERISA § 404(c) is appropriate given the fact that most 401(k) plans chose to elect designation as 404(c) plans. The allure of the 404(c) election is that it shifts the risk of investing to a plan's participants if all of the requirements of the section are met.

Unfortunately very few plans completely comply with 404(c)'s requirements. One study showed 94 percent of plans stating that they believed they were in full compliance with the 404(c) requirements. However Fred Reish, one of the nation's top ERISA attorneys, is on record as saying that he believes that as many as 90 percent of 404(c) plans are not compliant.# ERISA plan sponsors and other ERISA fiduciaries should take note of the potential consequences of false assumptions of 404(c) compliance, for as Reish points out

> our experience is that very few plans actually comply with 404(c).
> It is probable that most (perhaps as high as 90%) 401(k) plans do
> not comply with 404(c) and, as a result, the fiduciaries of those
> plans are personally responsible for the prudence of the investment decisions made by participants.

Another common area of liability for ERISA plan sponsors and other ERISA fiduciaries has to do with the proper evaluation, selection and monitoring of a plan's investment options. Most 401(k)/404(c) plans choose actively managed mutual funds as their plan's investment options. A recent study by noted financial professors Eugene Fama and Kenneth French found that only 3 percent of active managers produced returns that were able to cover their costs.

The Active Management Value Ratio™ (AMVR) metric discussed in this book provides a simple method for investment fiduciaries to analyze the prudence, or lack of prudence of an actively managed mutual fund. The AMVR only requires the ability to add and subtract a small amount of data, all of which is freely available online.

Experience has shown that in many cases, plan sponsors and investment committees lack the experience and/or knowledge to independently select investment options for their plans. Consequently, they blindly accept whatever information and evaluations their plan's service provider gives them.

The danger in that approach to managing a plan is that the courts have rejected that approach, ruling that while plan's are encouraged to seek the help of experts in selecting a plan's invest options when the plan lacks the experience and knowledge to do so on their own, plans may not blindly rely on the opinions of the expert opinions of third parties.

Plans and other ERISA fiduciaries employing third party investment experts, are required to take whatever advice a third party provides and then conduct their own thorough, independent and objective investigation. Furthermore, any reliance on such third party information and advice is only justified and reasonable if such advice is truly independent and impartial.

As one court pointed out in rejecting a plan's reliance on an insurance broker, third parties who receive compensation from another party can hardly be said to meet the "independent and impartial" requirement." Plan sponsors and other ERISA fiduciaries should take special note of the court's warning, as service providers are often affiliated with, and potentially receive compensation from, third party financial service firms such as securities broker-dealers and insurance companies, arguably negating the independent and impartial requirement.

APPENDIX D

Key Fiduciary Concepts and Decisions

<u>Note</u>: Some of these fiduciary decisions will reference ERISA. However, given the fact that ERISA is essentially a codification of the Restatement of Trust, they are equally applicable in non-ERISA fiduciary situations.

1. <u>High Standard for Fiduciary Duties</u>
Fiduciary duty creates the highest duty imposed by law.
Howard v. Shay, 100 F.3d 1484, 1488 (9th Cir. 1996)
Donovan v. Bierwirth, 680 F.2d 263, 272 n. 8 (2d Cir. 1982)

A trustee is held to something stricter than the morals of the market place. Not honesty alone, but the punctilio of an honor the most sensitive, is the standard of behavior....
Meinhard v. Salmon, 249 N.Y. 458, 464 (1928)

Good faith does not provide a defense to a claim of a breach of these fiduciary duties; "a pure heart and an empty head are not enough."
Donovan v. Cunningham, <u>716</u> F.2d <u>1455</u>, 1467 (5th Cir.1983)

2. <u>Fiduciary law based on common law of trusts</u>
Congress invoked the common law of trusts to define the general scope of the authority and responsibility of trustees and other fiduciaries.
Laborers Nat. Pension Fund v. Northern Trust Quantatative Advisors, 173 F.3d 313, 317 (5th Cir 1999)
Tibble v. Edison International, 135 S.Ct. 1823, 1828 (2015)
Donovan v. Mazzola, 716 F.2d 1226, 1231 (9th Cir. 1983)

3. <u>Fiduciary status</u>
Registered Investment Advisers:
S.E.C. v. Capital Gains Research Bureau, Inc., 375 U.S. 180, 194, 201 (1963)

Financial planners: Investment Advisory Rel. No.1092

Stockbrokers on discretionary accounts:
A discretionary account creates a relation of the most delicate fiduciary character.
Jenny v. Shearson, Hammill & Co., Inc.,
1981 U.S. Dist LEXIS 11469, Fed. Sec. L. Rep. (CCH) 97,911
(March 20, 1981)

Between the purely non-discretionary account and the purely discretionary account there is a hybrid-type account which plaintiff claims existed in this case. Such an account is one in which the broker has usurped actual control over a technically non-discretionary account. In such cases the courts have held that the broker, owes his customer the same fiduciary duties as he would have had the account been discretionary from the moment of its creation.
Leib v. Merrill Lynch, Pierce, Fenner & Smith, 461 F.Supp. 951, 954
(1978)

Control may be inferred from the broker-customer relationship when the customer lacks the ability to manage the account and must take the broker's word for what is happening....The issue is whether or not the customer, based on the information available and his ability to interpret it can independently evaluate his broker's suggestion.
Carras v. Burns, 516 F.2d 251 (4th Cir. 1975)
Follansbee v. Davis, Skaggs & Co., Inc., 681 F.2d 673, 676-77 (9th 1982)

4. **Dual registration and the fiduciary standard**
[When one acts simultaneously in the dual capacity of investment adviser and of broker and dealer,] conflicting interests must necessarily arise. When they arise, the law has consistently stepped in to provide safeguards in the form of proscribed and stringent standards of conduct on the part of the fiduciary. In this conflict of interest, the law wisely interposes.

It acts not on the possibility, that, in some cases, the sense of that duty may prevail over the motives of self-interest, but it provides against the probability in many cases, and the danger in all cases, that the dictates of

self-interest will exercise a predominant influence, and supersede that of duty.
Hughes v. S.E.C., 174 F.2d 969, 975 (D.C.C. 1949)

5. **Duty of Loyalty**
The most fundamental duty owed by the trustee to the beneficiaries of the trust is the duty of loyalty.... It is the duty of a trustee to administer the trust solely in the interest of the beneficiaries.
Pegram v. Herdrich, 530 U.S. 211, 120 S.Ct. 2143, 2151-52, 147 L.Ed.2d 164 (2000)
Moench v. Robertson, 62 F.3d 553, 561 (3d Cir.1995).

Eye single to the interests of the clients and beneficiaries.
Donovan v. Bierwirth, 680 F.2d 263 (2d Cir. 1982)
DiFelice v. U.S. Airways, 497 F.3d 410 (4th Cir. 2007)

6. **Duty to provide material information**
Duty to disclose material information is the core of ERISA fiduciary's responsibility.
Glaziers and Glassworkers Union Local No. 252 Annuity Fund v. Newbridge, 93 F.3d 1171 (3d. Cir. 1996)

ERISA imposes upon fiduciaries a general duty to disclose facts material to investment issues.
California Ironworkers Field Pension Trust v. Loomis Sayles & Co., 259 F.3d 1036 (CA 9 2001)

Failure to provide incomplete information about availability of comparable funds options that charged substantially lower fees was sufficient to state claim for breach of fiduciary duty of disclosure under ERISA.
In re Regions Morgan Keegan ERISA Litigation, 692 F. Supp 2d. 944 (W.D. Tenn. 2010)
Braden v. Wal-Mart Stores, Inc., 588 F.3d 585, 598-99 (8th Cir. 2009)

ERISA does not require participants to pursue third parties for information. A fiduciary cannot defend against a claim based on his or her failure to provide information on the claim by stating that the information is available elsewhere.

Chambers v. Kaleidoscope, Inc. Profit Sharing Plan and Trust, 650 F. Supp 359, 368 (N.D. Ga. 1986)

The duty to inform is a constant thread in the relationship between an ERISA fiduciary and trustee, it entails not only a negative duty not to misinform, but also an affirmative duty to inform the trustee knows that silence might be harmful.

In re Regions Morgan Keegan ERISA Litigation, 692 F. Supp 2d. 944 (W.D. Tenn. 2010)

Duty to disclose facts material to investment issues, even when a beneficiary has not specifically asked for the information.

Barker v. American Mobil Power Corp., 64 F.3d 1397, 1403 (1995). 12 F.3d 1292 (3d Cir. 1993)

7. **Duty of Prudence**

Wasting beneficiaries' money is imprudent. In devising and implementing strategies for the investment and management of trust assets, trustees are obliged to minimize costs.

Uniform Prudent Investor Act, §7, comment

[I]f fiduciaries imprudently evaluate, select, and monitor a plan's investment options, or do so for any purpose other than the best interest of the plan, they breach their fiduciary duties.

In re Regions Morgan Keegan ERISA Litigation, 692 F.Supp.2d 944, 957 (W.D. Tenn. 2010)

[T]he determination of whether an investment was objectively imprudent is made on the basis of what the [fiduciary] knew or should have known; and the latter necessarily involves consideration of what facts would have come to his attention if he had fully complied with his duty to investigate and evaluate.

Fink v. Nat'l Sav. and Trust Co., *772 F.2d 951, 962 (D.C.C. 1985)*

8. Duty to monitor third parties/appointees

[T]he power ...to appoint, retain and remove plan fiduciaries constitutes "discretionary authority" over the management or administration of a plan [results in fiduciary status for a plan]... Moreover, this authority carries with it a duty "to monitor appropriately" those subject to removal.
Coyne & Delany v. Selman, 98 F.3d 1457, 1465 (4th Cir. 1996)

The "ongoing responsibilities of a fiduciary who has appointed trustees" requires that [a]t reasonable intervals the performance of trustees and other fiduciaries should be reviewed by the appointing fiduciary in such a manner as may be reasonably expected to ensure that their performance has been in compliance with the *Liss v. Smith*, 991 F.Supp. 278, 311 (S.D.N.Y. 1998)

9. Duty to monitor investment options

[A] trustee's duties apply not only in making investments but also in monitoring and reviewing investments, which is to be
done in a manner that is reasonable and appropriate to the particular investments, courses of action, and strategies involved.... In short, under trust law, a fiduciary has a continuing duty of some kind to monitor investments and remove imprudent ones.
Tibble v. Edison International, 135 S.Ct. 1823, 1828-29 (2015)

The determination of whether an investment was objectively imprudent is made on the basis of what the trustee knew or should have known: and the latter necessarily involves consideration of what facts would have come to his attention if he had fully complied with his duty to investigate and evaluate."
Fink v. Nat'l Sav. and Trust Co, 772 F.2d 951, 962 (D.C.C. 1985)

Good faith does not provide a defense to a claim of a breach of fiduciary duties; a 'pure heart and an empty head' are not enough.
Donovan v. Cunningham, 716 F.2d 1455, 1467 (5th Cir. 1983).

82

Failure to utilize due care in selecting and monitoring a fund's service providers constitutes a breach of a trustees' fiduciary duty.
Liss v. Smith, 991 F. Supp. 278, 300 (S.D.N.Y. 1998)

10. Modern Portfolio Is ERISA's Standard for Prudence

[M]odern portfolio theory has been adopted in the investment community and, for the purposes of ERISA, However, the court may have overstated the appropriate relevance of modern portfolio theory to this case. Standing alone, it cannot provide a defense to the claimed breach of the "prudent man" duties here. Under ERISA, the prudence of investments or classes of investments offered by a plan must be judged individually. That is, a fiduciary must initially determine, and continue to monitor, the prudence of *each* investment option available to plan participants. Here the relevant "portfolio" that must be prudent is *each* available Fund considered on its own, including the Company Fund, not the full menu of Plan funds.
DiFelice v. U.S. Airways, 497 F.3d 410, 423 (4th Cir. 2007)
In re Unisys Sav. Plan Litigation, 74 F.3d 420, 438-41 (3d Cir. 1996).

Note: Many non-attorneys will read a legal decision and ignore the decisions notes. Investment fiduciaries should be sure to read note 8 in the decision, as the court notes a significant distinction between the use of MPT by fiduciaries. The court states that MPT can be used as a defense when fiduciary is selecting a single investment portfolio, such as a defined benefit plan, but MPT alone is not an acceptable defense when an imprudent fund is chosen as part of an available menu of investment options from which plan participants may *or may not* elect to combine with other investment options, such as a defined contribution plan.

11. Duty to Perform Independent Investigation

A fiduciary's independent investigation of the merits of a particular investment is at the heart of the prudent person standard.
U.S. v. Mason Tenders Dist. Council of Greater New York, 909 F.Supp. 882. 887 (S.D.N.Y. 1995)

Test of prudence largely in procedural terms, as whether the individual trustee, at the time they engaged in the challenged transactions, employed the appropriate methods to investigate the merits of the investment and to structure the investment.
Donovan v. Mazzola, 716 F.2d 1226, 1232 (9th Cir. 1983)

One extremely important factor is whether the expert advisor truly offers independent and impartial advice.
Gregg v. Transportation Workers of America Intern., 343 F.3d 833, 841 (6th Cir. 2003)

The failure to make any independent investigation and evaluation of a potential plan investment" has repeatedly been held to constitute a breach of fiduciary obligations.
Liss v. Smith, 991 F.Supp. 278, 298 (S.D.N.Y. 1998)
Fink v. Nat'l Savs. & Trust Co., 772 F.2d 951, 957 (D.C.C. 1984)

12. **Duty to seek help**

[W]here the trustees lack the requisite knowledge, experience and expertise to make the necessary decisions with respect to investments, their fiduciary obligations require them to hire independent professional advisors.
United States v. Mason Tenders Dist. Council of Greater New York, 909 F.Supp. 882, 886 (S.D.N.Y.1995)
Liss v. Smith, 991 F.Supp. 278, 296 (S.D.N.Y. 1998)

The trustee, nevertheless must make his own decision based on the expert's advice.
Donovan v. Mazzola, 716 F.2d 1226, 1234 (9th Cir. 1983)
Donovan v. Bierwirth, 680 F.2d 263, 272-73 (2d Cir. 1982)

13. **No blind reliance in third party advice**

Fiduciaries cannot blindly rely on third party advice. They must review, evaluate and understand the advice.
Howard v. Shay, 100 F.3d 1484, 1488 (9th Cir. 1996)

A determination whether a fiduciary's reliance on an expert advisor is justified is informed by many factors, including the expert's reputation and experience, the extensiveness and thoroughness of the expert's investigation, whether the expert's opinion is supported by relevant material, and whether the expert's methods and assumptions are appropriate to the decision at hand.

Bussian v. RJR Nabisco, Inc., 223 F.3d 286, 301 (5th Cir.2000)

14. Ignorance of Investments No Excuse

A trustee's lack of familiarity with investments is no excuse: under an objective standard trustees are to be judged 'according to the standards of others acting in a like capacity and familiar with such matters.

Katsaros v. Cody, 744 F.2d 270, 279 (2d Cir. 1984)

APPENDIX E

Variable Annuities: *Both Sides of the Story*

Variable annuities are one of the most overhyped, most oversold, and least understood investment products. A popular industry saying is that "annuities are sold, not bought." Variable annuity salesmen use various sales pitches to convince investors to purchase a variable annuity. However, as is often the case, what is unsaid is often as important, if not more important, than what is said. This information gap can have serious financial consequences for investors.

For purposes of this section, all references to variable annuities shall only refer to non-qualified variable annuities, those annuities that do not qualify for special treatment under the Internal Revenue Code.

Basic Structure of Annuities

Before analyzing some of the popular sales pitches used by variable annuity salesmen, it is important to understand the basic structure of a variable annuity. A variable annuity can be described as an insurance contract wrapped around mutual fund-like subaccounts. The presence of the insurance "wrapper" allows the variable annuity to provide tax-deferred growth.

Variable annuities typically charge two primary fees, an annual insurance fee and an annual subaccount management fee. The insurance fee usually consists of a mortality and expense (M& E) charge, usually in the range of 1.25-1.4 percent of the accumulated value of the variable annuity, and an administrative fee, usually in the range of 0.15-0.20 percent of the accumulated value of the variable annuity.

The M&E charge covers the guaranteed death benefit (GDB), which ensures that in the event that the owner of the variable annuity dies before annuitizing the variable annuity, his/her heirs will receive no less than the amount that the owner had invested in the variable annuity. The M&E charge also covers commission payments and general overhead expenses.

The subaccount management fee is charged for the professional management of the subaccount, much like the annual management fee charged by mutual funds. Subaccount management fees can vary depending on the type of account, with management fees typically falling within the 0.80-1.00 percent range.

The total annual fee charged on most variable annuities is approximately 2 percent of the overall value of the variable annuity. When compared to an average annual fee of 1 percent for actively managed mutual funds, 0.45 percent for passively managed mutual funds, and the typically low annual fees for exchange traded funds (ETFs), it is easy to see why the high fees and expenses associated with variable annuities are criticized, especially when their drag on long term performance is factored in.

Annuity Sales Pitches
So why do people continue to invest in variable annuities? Remember, annuities are sold, not bought. An analysis of some of the sales pitches used by variable annuity salesmen, in terms of what is said and what is unsaid, may prove helpful.

What's said: "Variable annuities offer tax deferred growth."
What's unsaid: There are a number of investment accounts (e.g., 401(k) accounts, IRA accounts, Keogh accounts, SIMPLE accounts) that offer tax deferred growth without the high fees and expenses associated with variable annuities. Even investors in stocks, mutual funds, and ETFs can achieve virtual tax-deferred growth as long as they do not actively trade their accounts and they choose investments with low turnover rates (e.g., passively managed funds such as index funds) and low income pay-outs.

The value of the tax-deferred growth offered by variable annuities is reduced by the effect of the high fees and expenses associated with variable annuities. Various studies have been done comparing the cost of investing in variable annuities to the cost of investing in mutual funds.

These studies have generally concluded that in most cases it takes a minimum of 15-20 years, in some cases over forty years, for the owner of a variable annuity to break-even from the fees and expenses of variable annuities. In some cases, the owner of the variable annuity may never break-even.

An article by Dr. William Reichenstein of Baylor University provides an excellent in-depth analysis of the effects of fees on the overall return realized by variable annuity and mutual fund investors. Among Dr. Reichenstein's findings: (1) that costs have a significant effect on the overall effectiveness of an investment, (2) that low cost mutual funds and low cost annuities are the most effective investments for investors, and (3) that the typical variable annuity, with a fee of 2 percent or more and an annual contract fee of $20-$30, is the least effective investment for investors.

The value of the tax-deferred growth offered by variable annuities is also reduced by the tax aspects of a variable annuity as compared to a mutual fund. Tax-deferred does not mean tax-free. Sooner or later, the variable annuity owner or his/her beneficiaries will have to pay income tax on the capital appreciation within the variable annuity.

Mutual fund owners can often use the capital gains tax rates to reduce the taxes on their mutual funds. Variable annuity owners cannot use the capital gains tax rate, as disbursements from variable annuities are taxed as ordinary income, which usually results in more tax liability and less money for the variable annuity owner or his/her beneficiaries.

What's said: "You don't pay sales charges when you purchase a variable annuity, so all of your money goes to work for you, unlike mutual funds that charge front-end sales charges, and stocks and ETFs, which require an investor to pay brokerage commissions."
What's Unsaid: There are excellent no-load mutual funds that perform as well as, and often better than, variable annuity subaccounts.

These no-load mutual funds usually charge annual management fees far less that those charged for variable annuity sub-accounts, especially passively managed mutual funds such as index funds. Investors purchasing stocks and ETFs can use discount brokers to greatly reduce the amount of any brokerage commissions.

The statement that variable annuity owners pay no sales charges, while technically correct, can be somewhat misleading. Variable annuity salesmen do receive a commission for each variable annuity they sell, such commission usually being in the range of 6-7 percent of the total amount invested in the variable annuity. While a purchaser of a variable annuity is not directly assessed a front-end sales charge or a brokerage commission, the variable annuity owner does reimburse the insurance company for the commission that was paid. The primary source of such reimbursement is through the variable annuity's various fees and charges, particularly the M&E charge.

To ensure that the cost of commissions paid is recovered, the insurance company typically imposes surrender charges on a variable annuity owner who tries to cash out of the variable annuity before the expiration of a certain period of time. The terms of these surrender charges vary, but a typical surrender charge schedule might provide for an initial surrender charge of 7 percent for withdrawals during the first year, decreasing 1 percent each year thereafter until the eighth year, when the surrender charges would end. Some surrender charge schedules that charge a flat rate, such as 7 percent, over the entire surrender charge period.

One recent variable annuity innovation that has caused regulators a great deal of concern has been the so-called "bonus" annuities. These products are marketed in such a way that the public may believe that they receive a free bonus, usually in the range of 3-4 percent of their investment, upon their purchase of the annuity.

In truth, the insurance company sponsoring the bonus annuity simply increases the term and/or the amount of the surrender charges to recover the "bonus." These bonus annuities continue to be scrutinized due to their potential to mislead and deceive the public into thinking that they are receiving something that they really are not receiving.

Prospective annuity purchasers should always study the surrender charge schedule to minimize potential costs. Since surrender charge schedules often reflect the amount of commissions paid to the variable annuity salesman, an investor can compare the commission paid on a variable annuity (typically 6-7 percent) and the commission charged by front-end load mutual funds (typically 4-5 percent).

What's said: "Variable annuities offer a guaranteed death benefit (GDB) that ensures that the variable annuity owner's heirs will get no less than the amount of money that the variable annuity owner invested in the variable annuity."

What's unsaid: Most variable annuities discontinue the GDB once the variable annuity owner reaches a certain age. Furthermore, a variable annuity owner also generally loses the GDB if the owner elects to annuitize the variable annuity in order to receive the guaranteed lifetime income benefits.

The value of the GDB itself is questionable. Variable annuities are intended to be long term investments. Given the long term historical performance of the stock market, it is highly unlikely that a variable annuity owner will need to use the GDB since, over the long term, the accumulated value of the variable annuity will probably exceed the amount of the GDB. In his article, Dr. Reichenstein refers to studies that have estimated that the GDB is worth approximately 0.087 percent or less[2], although insurance companies currently impose M & E charges in the range to 1.25%-1.4 percent to cover their GDB liability.

Another interesting fact about the M & E charge is that while the GDB in most variable annuities only insures the variable annuity owner's investment in the variable annuity, the principal, the M&E charge is calculated based upon the accumulated value of the of the variable annuity, which includes both the principal and all capital appreciation within the annuity.

This would seem to be clearly inequitable to the variable annuity owner who is forced to pay a higher amount of M & E charges as the value of the variable annuity increases, with no corresponding increase in the insurance company's obligation to the variable annuity owner.

For an additional fee, some insurance companies do offer a benefit that steps-up the amount of the GDB to the overall value of the variable annuity on certain anniversary dates. Given the unlikely need to use the GDB, the value of yet another layer of cost is equally questionable.

What's said: "Variable annuities can provide a lifetime stream of income, guaranteeing that you'll never run out of money to live on."
What's unsaid: To get the lifetime stream of income, the variable annuity owner generally has to annuitize the variable annuity. Upon annuitization, the variable annuity owner will receive a monthly payment, with the amount of the payment being based upon the owner's age and the settlement option that was chosen. The decision to annuitize should only be made after consideration of all of the consequences of such a decision.

Upon annuitization, the variable annuity owner gives up control of the annuity's assets. Even more important, depending on the settlement options offered by the insurance company and the settlement option chosen by the variable annuity owner, once the variable annuity is annuitized the insurance company, not the owner's heirs, will receive any money left in the annuity when the owner dies.

Some variable annuities may require the owner of a variable annuity to annuitize their annuity upon reaching a certain age. Prospective variable annuity purchasers should always check the terms of a variable annuity being considered to see if the annuity contains such forced annuitization language, as it could frustrate an investor's estate plans.

Annuitization is, in essence, a gamble. The insurance company is hoping that the variable annuity owner dies before depleting all of the assets in the annuity, in which case the insurance company may receive the balance remaining in the annuity. The annuity owner, on the other hand, is gambling that they will live long enough to deplete the assets in their annuity.

What's said: "You can rollover money over from your 401(k) or other retirement account into an IRA and then purchase a variable annuity for such account. You'll continue to receive tax deferred growth of your money and you'll get the safety of the guaranteed death benefit."
What's unsaid: Qualified plans and IRAs already offer tax deferred growth. Consequently, purchasing a variable annuity within an IRA simply adds the high fees and expenses of the variable annuity without providing the investor with any meaningful additional benefits.

Many people work hard during their lifetime to accumulate funds not only for their retirement, but also to create an estate to leave to their heirs. Annuitization can result in an insurance company, not one's heirs, inheriting the results of one's hard work. While IRA owners must begin to take disbursements from an IRA once they reach a certain age, the balance remaining in the IRA at the owner's death passes to their designated beneficiaries. There are also various ways to minimize the amount of the required disbursements from an IRA so that the IRA assets can benefit one's children, grandchildren and beyond.

Placing a variable annuity within an IRA may result in a forced annuitization because of the required disbursements from an IRA at 70½ or because of language in the variable annuity requiring annuitization at a certain age or upon the occurrence of some event. Such a forced annuitization may result in consequences unintended, and undesired, by the IRA owner, including the owner's heirs' loss of their inheritance.

The questionable value of the GDB has already been discussed. The GDB is simply insurance. An investor who needs insurance and the GDB it provides should buy insurance, but through more cost effective options, such as term insurance.

What's said: "You'll have access to your money at all times since variable annuities typically allow an owner to withdraw up to 10% from their annuity annually, after the first year, without any penalty."
What's unsaid: The insurance company's decision to waive any penalties does not change the fact that all withdrawals from a variable annuity result in tax consequences.

Withdrawal of gains from variable annuities are taxed as ordinary income. Variable annuity owners cannot use the capital gains tax rates to reduce their tax liability. In addition, withdrawals made by an owner prior to reaching the age of 59½ are generally subject to a penalty tax equal to 10% of the amount withdrawn.

Many variable annuities allow an owner to withdraw more than 10% in a limited number of circumstances. In the event that unanticipated circumstances arise during the period that the variable annuity's surrender charges are applicable, and such circumstances are not among those specified for allowing withdrawals beyond the insurance company's annual allowance, the variable annuity owner may have to pay the applicable surrender charges in addition to the ordinary income and penalty taxes.

<u>What's said</u>: "If you're ever dissatisfied with the performance of your variable annuity, you can switch to another variable annuity without paying any taxes."

<u>What's unsaid</u>: Tax-free exchanges, known as "1035 exchanges," present a number of issues. Both the FINRA and the SEC have made questionable variable annuity sales tactics, including 1035 exchanges, a priority.

There are reports that 1035 exchanges account for a significant portion of annual variable annuity sales.[3] Brokers and advisors like 1035 exchanges since they result in new commissions for the broker or the advisor. Variable annuity owners contemplating such an exchange should note that any 1035 exchange made while the existing variable annuity is subject to surrender charges will result in the owner having to pay such surrender charges.

In addition, if the new variable annuity imposes surrender charges, those surrender charges begin anew. Consequently, prior to making a 1035 exchange, a variable annuity owner whose annuity is free of surrender charges should carefully consider the costs and the limitations that new surrender charges may create.

Generally speaking, a variable annuity owner should only consider making a 1035 exchange if (1) the existing annuity is not subject to any surrender charges, and (2) the existing variable annuity is being exchanged for a new annuity that has low or no surrender charges and lower fees and expenses than the existing variable annuity. Owners of variable annuities issued prior to 1982 should consult with a tax expert prior to making a 1035 exchange due to the special tax issues associated with such annuities.

<u>What's said</u>: "If you're ever dissatisfied with the performance of a subaccount in your variable annuity, you can switch to another subaccount without having to pay sales loads or taxes."

<u>What's unsaid</u>: While a mutual fund investor can choose from the entire universe of mutual funds, the variable annuity owner is limited to those subaccounts that are offered within the variable annuity.

Some variable annuities offer twenty or more subaccounts, while others may offer ten or less. In some cases, the insurance company sponsoring the variable annuity may limit all, or a majority, of the available subaccounts to their proprietary products. Quite often, these proprietary products have less than stellar performance records. It should also be noted that some variable annuities do impose a fee, usually in the range of $20-25 per switch, if the variable annuity owner exceeds a certain number of sub-account switches in a year.

What's said: "The tax deferred growth offered by a variable annuity will allow you to pass more money on to your heirs."
What's unsaid: Variable annuities are terrible estate planning tools. If the variable annuity is ever annuitized, the variable annuity owner loses control of the annuity's assets and, depending on the settlement options offered and chosen, the insurance company, not the owner's heirs, may get any money remaining in the annuity when the owner dies.

If the variable annuity owner never annuitizes the annuity, then his/her heirs do receive the value of the variable annuity at the owner's death. The beneficiaries of a variable annuity must pay income tax on the portion of the proceeds that represent the capital appreciation within the annuity. Such proceeds are taxed as ordinary income instead of capital gains, generally resulting in higher taxes and significantly less money for the owner's beneficiaries.

Heirs who receive mutual funds, stocks, and ETFs as their inheritances pay no taxes due to the step-up in basis these investment products receive upon an owner's death. The value of this estate planning benefit cannot be overstated, as it allows heirs to avoid the taxes associated with variable annuities and allows the owner to accomplish his/her goal, namely to pass more of the estate to his/her heirs.

Equity Indexed Annuities
Much has been written about the advantages of investing in index funds. Index funds became even more popular during the bull market of the late 80's and the 90's, as indexes regularly reported annual double-digit gains.

The annuity industry quickly responded by offering a fixed-income annuities whose returns were based on the performance of an underlying
stock market index, such as the S&P 500. The annuities go by various
names including equity indexed annuities.

While equity indexed annuities are technically fixed, rather than variable,
annuities, they merit discussion due to the fact that they are tied to an equity market index. Some might say that the marketing of equity indexed
annuities can mislead the public due to the severe restrictions placed on
the indexed annuity owner's ability to fully participate in an index's gain.

Most equity-indexed annuities limit, or "cap," the owner's annual gain to
10-12 percent regardless of the index's actual gain. The owner's ability to
participate in the index's gain is further restricted by the imposition of a
"participation rate," typically in the range of 70-80 percent. For example,
if an investor owned an equity indexed annuity that capped the annuity
owner's annual gain at 10 percent, with a participation rate of 70 percent,
the most that the annuity owner could earn for that year would be 7 percent (10 percent x .70), even if the index actually gained 30 percent that
year.

Some equity-indexed annuities do offer downside protection by guaranteeing a minimum annual return, usually related to prevailing interest
rates. Nevertheless, when an investor in an index based product is limited
to a gain of 7 percent when the index itself shows a much larger gain, it is
easy to understand why some investors may question the inherent value
and fairness of the product.

Riders
Most annuities offer the owner a variety of additional benefits in exchange for additional fees. These benefits are offered in the form of additional contract provisions, or "riders." The number of riders is too large to
allow a complete discussion here. The prospective investor should analyze each rider offered to determine the true value of the benefit, if any,
being offered and the effect of the additional fees.

One rider currently being offered is called an "enhanced death benefit" (EDB). The lack of a stepped-up basis for variable annuities is often an impediment to their purchase. In an effort to counter this disadvantage, the EDB pays an additional amount of money to the heirs in an attempt to mitigate the effect of the ordinary income tax that they must pay. The value of the EDB is very questionable due to the way that it is calculated and the fact that the EDB itself is also taxable. More often than not, the variable annuity owner will determine that the benefit offered by the rider simply does not justify the added cost of the rider.

Decisions

Do variable annuities ever make sense? One situation where a variable annuity may make sense is where an investor wants tax-deferred growth and they have maxed out all other tax-deferred growth options, such as 401(k)s and IRAs. Another situation where variable annuities may make sense is a situation where one's profession and/or financial situation suggest a need for asset protection and the investor resides in a state that grants annuities protection against creditors.

Even then, an investors and investment fiduciaries should only consider a variable annuity with low annual fees and little or no surrender charges, such as those offered by Vanguard, T. Rowe Price and TIAA-CREF, and only invest money that they can leave invested for a long time. Prospective annuity purchaser should remember Dr. Reichenstein's findings that the typical variable annuity sold by variable annuity salesmen, with annual fees and expenses of approximately 2 percent and an annual contract fee are always a poor investment choice.[4] Investors should also look at the number and the type of subaccounts offered within the variable annuity, the performance record of each subaccount, and the annual management fee charged by the subaccounts

What options are available to investors who already own a variable annuity and are either dissatisfied with the performance of their annuity or question whether an annuity was a suitable investment for them? The question of suitability depends on various factors such as the investor's age, investment objectives, financial needs, risk tolerance level, income, and need for liquidity. Suitability determinations are best handled by a truly objective source such as an attorney or a fee-only financial planner who has a background in annuities or securities compliance.

If a determination is made that the annuity was an unsuitable investment for the investor, the investor may choose to contact the broker and brokerage firm that sold them the annuity, as well as the insurance company that sponsors the annuity, and request that the variable annuity contract be rescinded and that their original investment be refunded in full.

Given the investigations by FINRA and the SEC into questionable annuity sales practices, the sanctions that have already been assessed in some cases, and pending legal actions involving the sale of annuities, investors with suitability questions should consider seeking a professional evaluation and objective advice regarding their situation to ensure that they are not exposing themselves to unnecessary financial losses due to unsuitable investments.

Variable annuity owners whose annuity was suitable, but who are dissatisfied with the costs and/or the performance of their annuity should consider exchanging their annuity for an annuity with lower costs, low or no surrender charges, and/or a better performance record once the surrender charge period on their present annuity expires. Annuity exchanges involving annuities that are still subject to surrender charges are generally discouraged due to the loss that would be created in having to pay the surrender charges.

Ethics and Fiduciary Issues

The marketing and sale of variable annuities continues to be a hot topic with regulators. By law, brokers are only supposed to recommend products that are suitable for an investor given their investment objectives, financial needs and overall investment profile. Investment advisors are required to put a client's interests first and only recommend actions that are in a client's best interests.

Unfortunately, regulators continue to find far too many cases where the brokers and advisors have failed to honor these obligations and have engaged in predatory sales and marketing practices. In fact, annuity salesmen are sometimes taught to use such predatory tactics to induce an investor to purchase a variable annuity.[5]

As more and more variable annuity owners figure out the trap of annuitization, fewer variable annuity owners are annuitizing their contracts. This reduction in the annuitization rate has serious implications for the insurance industry, as it means that the amount of money that they receive from annuitized variable annuities could be significantly reduced. To prevent this loss, variable annuity owners should be alert to brokers and advisors urging more of their variable annuity clients to annuitize their variable annuities.

Given the fact that annuitization can frustrate a variable annuity owner's estate plans and that there are other options available, such as systematic withdrawals, that enable variable annuity owners to tap into their variable annuity without forfeiting control of their annuity, a recommendation to annuitize may not be in a client's best interests. In such circumstances, a recommendation to annuitize could raise ethical questions and involve possible violations of securities laws/regulations.

Another example of the variable annuity industry's seeming indifference to the best interests of the client can be seen in stories and reports prepared or sponsored by the industry comparing investments in annuities to investments in mutual funds. Close analysis of such stories and reports usually reveal that the opinions are based on assumptions heavily favoring the annuities, such as assuming that investors will only invest in mutual funds with high fees and that the fund and/or the investor will generate substantial capital gains by heavily trading the fund/account. Without such assumptions, the chances that the variable annuity will outperform the mutual fund are greatly reduced. Inexperienced investors, however, may not be able to detect such biases.

Rarely, if ever, will you find an industry-prepared or industry-sponsored analysis comparing an investment in a variable annuity to an investment in a low cost mutual fund, particularly an index fund. The low annual fees and passive management associated with index funds virtually guarantee that the variable annuity will always lose out in such comparisons.

Long-term owners of stocks and ETFs could also outperform variable annuities as well since the stocks and ETFs would not be burdened by high annual fees and annual capital gains. A failure to disclose such relevant information may also raise ethical questions, particularly if the broker or advisor has a fiduciary relationship with the client.

Such issues, combined with dubious practices such as recommending the purchase of variable annuities within qualified plans and IRAs, recommending unsuitable annuity exchanges, and "bonus" annuities, raise legitimate questions as to whether recommendations to purchase variable annuities are based on the client's best interests or the fact that commissions paid for variable annuity sales are higher than most other investment options. Unfortunately, FINRA and SEC investigations have proven that far too often the motivating factor is the latter.

Regulators have limited resources to detect and address abusive variable annuity practices. Consequently, investors must assume greater responsibility for their investment decisions and be willing to stand up for their rights when they have been misled or have suffered financial losses due to unsuitable investment advice.

Conclusion

Variable annuities are simply not an effective investment choice for most investors due to the costs, restrictions and adverse tax aspects of the product, particularly when compared to other investment options such as mutual funds and ETFs. Variable annuities are an especially poor choice as estate planning tools, as the implications of annuitization, the lack of a stepped-up basis at the variable annuity owner's death, and the unavailability of the capital gains tax to minimize taxes may actually prevent a variable annuity owner from effectively passing on his/her estate to his/her heirs.

Variable annuities are investment products that are complex and often misunderstood. The lack of available information and the multitude of options and riders usually offered in connection with variable annuities only serve to increase the confusion. Prospective variable annuity purchasers should carefully consider both what is said and what is unsaid in sales pitches for variable annuities before deciding to invest in such products.

Investors who do decide to purchase a variable annuity should only consider those with low annual fees, low or no surrender charges, and an adequate number of quality subaccounts to allow them to realize the highest returns possible. Owners of variable annuities should use systematic withdrawals, rather than annuitization, if they need to withdraw money from the variable annuity in order to ensure that the owner's heirs, not the insurance company, receive the value of the variable annuity upon the owner's death.

Notes

1. W. Reichenstein, "Who Should Buy A Nonqualified Tax-Deferred Annuity," Financial Services Review, Vol. 11, No. 1, (Spring 2002), p.30. (with permission)
2. Ibid.
3. J. Opdyke, Shifting Annuities May Help Brokers More Than Investors, Wall St. J., Feb. 16, 2001, at C1.
4. Reichenstein, at 30.
5. E. Schultz and J. Opdyke, Annuities 101: How to Sell to Senior Citizens, Wall St. J., July 2, 2002, at C1.

Recommended Reading

C.T. Geer, "The Great Annuity Rip-off," Forbes, February 9, 1998.

J. Kalter, "Annuities: Just Say No," Worth, July/August 1996.
National Association of Security Dealers, "FINRA Investor Alert: Should You Exchange Your Variable Annuity?" February 15, 2001, available on the Internet at www.FINRAr.com/alert_02_ 01.htm.

S. Burns, "Why Variable Annuities Are No Match for Index Funds," available on the Internet at moneycentral.msn.com/ articles/invest/ extra/7272.asp.

About the Author

Mr. Watkins is the Founder and CEO/Managing Member of InvestSense, LLC, an investment education firm that provides wealth management programs and forensic risk management programs to individuals, pension plans, educational institutions and other groups, including strategies for the accumulation, preservation/protection, distribution and recovery of wealth.

Mr. Watkins had over twenty years of experience in the area of investment quality of advice issues. He has served as a compliance officer/ director for various broker-dealers. He served as the initial director of the Peer Review Department at the Certified Financial Planner Board of Standards and later as the Director of Financial Planning Quality Assurance for AXA Advisors,

He is a 1981 graduate of the University of Notre Dame Law School and an honors graduate from Georgia State University. He is a member of Omicron Delta Kappa National Honor Society. He is an Eagle Scout and a recipient of scouting's God and Country Award.

He has been an attorney since 1981 and is a member of the Fiduciary Section of the State Bar of Georgia. He has extensive experience in the areas of fiduciary oversight, financial planning, asset protection/wealth preservation, fiduciary law, securities/ investment law and estate planning. He has earned both the CERTIFIED FINANCIAL PLANNER™ designation and the Accredited Wealth Management Advisor^{SM} designation from the College of Financial Planning. He serves as a CFP® Ambassador on behalf of the Certified Financial Planner Board of Standards.

Mr. Watkins is the owner of two blogs - "CommonSense InvestSense," an informational and educational blog for investors, and "The Prudent Investment Adviser Rules," a blog for investment advisers and other investment professionals. Mr. Watkins has written numerous articles on the subject of investing, wealth management, wealth preservation, asset protection, and 401(k)/pension law. His work has appeared on, and he has been quoted on, sites such as the Huffington Post, financialplanning.com, and institutional investor.com.

Specialties: Quality of Investment Advice Analysis; Fiduciary Oversight Services; Fiduciary Law and Consulting; Fiduciary Audits; Wealth Management, Preservation, and Recovery Strategies; Litigation Settlement Consulting; 401k/403b Compliance Consulting; Asset Protection Planning; Retirement Distribution Planning; Estate Planning; Securities/RIA Compliance Consulting; and Securities Litigation Support

Mr. Watkins online:

Email: investsensellc@gmail.com

LinkedIn: https://www.linkedin.com/in/jw3investsensellc.com

Twitter: @investsense

Blogs: "CommonSense InvestSense": investsense.com

"The Prudent Investment Adviser Rule": iainsight.wordpress.com

www.ingramcontent.com/pod-product-compliance
Lightning Source LLC
Chambersburg PA
CBHW060355190526
45169CB00002B/606